Citizens Yet Strangers

CITIZENS
YET
STRANGERS

Living Authentically Catholic in a Divided America

Kenneth Craycraft

Our Sunday Visitor
Huntington, Indiana

Nihil Obstat
Msgr. Michael Heintz, Ph.D.
Censor Librorum

Imprimatur
✠ Kevin C. Rhoades
Bishop of Fort Wayne-South Bend
September 25, 2023

The *Nihil Obstat* and *Imprimatur* are official declarations that a book is free from doctrinal or moral error. It is not implied that those who have granted the *Nihil Obstat* and *Imprimatur* agree with the contents, opinions, or statements expressed.

Our Sunday Visitor Publishing Division
Our Sunday Visitor, Inc.
200 Noll Plaza
Huntington, IN 46750
www.osv.com
1-800-348-2440

ISBN: 978-1-63966-081-0 (Inventory No. T2817)
1. RELIGION—Christianity—Catholic.
2. RELIGION—Religion, Politics & State.
3. RELIGION—Christian Living—Social Issues.
eISBN: 978-1-63966-082-7
LCCN: 2023948530

Cover design: Tyler Ottinger
Interior design: Amanda Falk
Cover art: AdobeStock

PRINTED IN THE UNITED STATES OF AMERICA

In Memoriam

Fr. Ernest L. Fortin and Fr. Matthew L. Lamb,

*who taught me to look more closely
and read more carefully*

Contents

Introduction

In the midst of rapidly changing social norms, the challenges of Catholic public witness in the United States have become increasingly more difficult and frustrating. If you picked up this book, you probably already know that. What might not be as obvious, however, is why we Catholics are so ill equipped to meet these social challenges, or even to articulate a response to them. Making matters worse, Catholics can be found on both sides of polarizing cultural and political issues, each side thinking theirs is the only possible position for a Catholic to hold. We cannot even convince our fellow Catholics of the rationale for our contradictory policy positions. If we cannot communicate with other Catholics, it should be no surprise when we find ourselves mute against the broader culture. The purpose of this book is to address this precarious situation as a symptom of the same basic problem: namely, that we have abandoned (or forgotten) the moral language of Catholicism and replaced it with a moral dialect that leads inevitably to failure and frustration. We find it difficult to respond to non-Catholic or secular positions on specific policy issues because we have largely accepted the basic moral anthropology — the nature and purpose of the human person — of those alien points of view. In other words, we have assented to foundational moral principles that give away the game before it even begins. Having conceded the fundamental moral theory, we find it difficult to articulate a justification for alternative practices. For example, Catholics almost universally argue that abortion is immoral because it infringes the "right to life" of the unborn child. We have largely accepted that the language of individual subjective rights is the proper way to frame the argument. But then we are at a loss to explain why the rights of the unborn child should prevail over those of the woman who considers that child to be an intrusion on her own rights. We accept the basic moral philosophy that informs the cant "My body, my choice," so we should not be surprised when we cannot win the debate by promoting the rights of the unborn baby against her right to bodily autonomy. When such basic moral categories as inalienable subjective individual rights conflict, whose rights should prevail? And on what grounds?

This problem is not limited to Catholic interactions with non-Catholics. Some "pro-choice" Catholics argue that their Catholic opponents advocate arbitrary limits to the scope of the subjective rights of women that they otherwise endorse. This is because both sides have informed their basic moral positions from the same non-Catholic source, but have refined particular policy positions in terms of American partisan loyalty. Put another way, Catholics find it difficult to speak to one another because we have allowed ourselves to be informed by one of the two dominant variations of American liberalism, as found in the two dominant political parties in the United States. Both these parties accept the same basic individualist principles, but differ on the details of how they should be applied. This is the anthropology most U.S. Catholics accept, rather than a truly Catholic understanding of the human person. Catholics on one side are happy with the practical implications of this individualist theory. Catholics on the other side are unhappy with those implications, but are so thoroughly embedded in the theory that they cannot articulate a coherent practical alternative to them. And so we just raise our voices.

American Catholics have largely been formed by the liberal story of America rather than the biblical story of Catholic Christianity. We don't want to live in conflict with the moral and political theory that has formed American politics, law, and culture, so we have tried to find an articulation of faith that is compatible with American liberal ideals. As a result, we have collapsed faith into the same political continuum of liberalism, and we have staked out opposing positions on one of its two extremes. We share the faith of American liberalism but differ on its implications.

It is not my intention to cast blame for this situation, or to make judgments in favor of one side against the other. In many ways, this state of affairs is unsurprising and even sympathetic. Catholics want to live peaceably as American citizens, so we embrace and endorse the moral and political ideas that define and delimit what that means. We see the tension between faith and politics, to use shorthand, and think that we must find a resolution to the tension. And we have. But the cost has been the integrity of our own theological language and witness.

In one sense, of course, this problem of the relationship of Catholicism to cultural, civic, and political identification is not new. Indeed, it is as old as Christianity itself. While contemporary debates do seem to be especially contentious, the problems that underlie them are inherent in the very nature of Catholic faith and practice. Indeed, Catholic discipleship is routinely described in expressly political terms: Christ the King, Mary Queen of Heaven, God on his throne. These political terms suggest that Catholics are subservient to authority that is potentially in tension with, if not contradicted by, other politics. This tension was at the heart of late nineteenth-century anti-Catholic legislation and political rhetoric in the United States, characterized by such things as the rise of so-called Blaine statutes and amendments, and the editorial cartoons of people like Thomas Nast.

In response to these anti-Catholic movements — to show that we can be good American citizens — Catholics gradually ceded the moral arguments that divide Catholic witness from American identity. To be accepted by the liberal and Protestant American culture, we have unwittingly accepted the basic moral premises that formed the culture. In the process, however, we have forgotten the theologies and practices that separate being Catholic from being a certain kind of American. In other words, our response to those who say that Catholics cannot be good Americans is to accept the moral theory that informs being a good American, while thinking we can still maintain adherence to moral principles that are not consistent with that theory.

Thus Catholics in the United States have difficulty even talking to one another in an authentically Catholic dialect. The typical American Catholic is more comfortable talking to a non-Catholic person with whom he identifies politically than with a another Catholic. We lack a coherent moral and political vocabulary, which means that we have little hope of articulating principles of freedom and common good to the broader culture, because we don't even know what that looks like within the Church.

This is the case for at least two reasons: First, we have forgotten the language of the Catholic moral life. Second, we have reduced moral commitments to political identity, and political identity to party loyalty. Thus our moral and political lives are more likely formed by partisan identification than Catholic discipleship. We have reduced our moral lives to our partisan loyalties to such a degree that that we think that they are the same thing as Christian discipleship.

My goal in this book is to challenge all of us to recover a Catholic moral language through what are sometimes called the "four pillars" of Catholic social doctrine: human dignity, the common good, subsidiarity, and solidarity. Each of these principles can be learned as a better way to think about social and civic issues, including legal, political, economic, and regulatory matters. From abortion to immigration; from health care to capital punishment; from contraception to euthanasia, we Catholics have a moral language that is richer, deeper, and more comprehensive than the language of liberal Protestantism to which we so often unwittingly default. More importantly, and in contrast to these various liberal Protestant dialects, the language of Catholic social doctrine upholds the moral anthropology at the heart of the Catholic understanding of the human person.

We must begin to recover a moral language that is formed by Catholic moral doctrine rather than by liberal political theory. I am fully aware that it may be a quixotic effort. But the effort is worth the hope that we Catholics might once again be a witness to the integrity of faith, rather than participants in its demise.

Chapter 1

We Are All Liberal Protestants

Catholics in the United States today are liberal Protestants be- fore we are anything else. To form our moral lives as Cath- olics is a constant battle to overcome the liberal Protestantism that we began to consume with our mother's milk.

Now, by *liberal*, I do not mean the way that someone on the left end of the spectrum of American politics would identify himself (or by which others would identify him). Rather, I mean the basic moral anthropology that animates the whole political spectrum in the United States, from the far left of the Democrat- ic Party to the far right of the Republican Party. This anthropol- ogy is characterized by at least two elements: (1) radical person- al autonomy and (2) an absolute commitment to individualism, characterized by the language of "individual rights" as the basic moral foundation (or, indeed, for some the only measure of moral action). As I explain in chapter 3, these two elements are not only contrary to the Catholic understanding of the human person, but corrosive of Catholic faith and witness.

Defined this way, the overwhelming majority of Americans are liberals, whether of the left/progressive or right/conservative variety. These are merely variations on a theme — disagreements within the family. When I use the term *liberal* (or *liberalism*) throughout this book, I am not referring to what we usually regard as the political left, or the Democratic Party. Rather, I am referring to the political theory that forms and informs the moral and political lives of virtually all Americans. In this theory, every human relationship is reduced to contractual agreements (whether implicit or explicit) by autonomous moral actors. This is another way of saying that the human person is naturally individual and isolated from every other human person.

In this liberal view, the human person is not naturally social, and thus there are no natural social institutions. Rather, all human associations are conventional — formed by the agreement of autonomous individuals in voluntary institutions. Human associations are mere contractual transactions, entered into from positions of radical autonomy. "Community" is nothing more than a series of mutual agreements to forgo some of our absolute rights for the sake of our own safety. And because all institutions are voluntary and contractual, there is no moral obligation to conform to them, other than the mutual agreement itself.

This includes the Church.

Even well-meaning Catholics in the United States have a tendency to identify the Church as one voluntary institution among others, created by the wills of her members, who are not answerable to the Church beyond the extent that they choose. We also have a tendency to think of the Church as making moral admonitions and encouragements, but with no more purchase on our moral commitments than we decide to give her. This is because we reduce morality to individual subjective rights, which encompass every moral question. Thus, like actual Protestants, our commitment to the moral teaching of the Church is mere coincidence. We reserve our actual personal commitment to our individual conscience, which is independent from any authoritative magisterium.

For many American Catholics, the individual's conscience — in both its formation and application — always trumps the Church's teaching. In turn, the Church's teaching is seen as nothing more than a list of options to which one may consent (or not) without any scruple as to one's standing in the Church. When we do agree with the Church's teaching, that is nothing more than serendipity. When we disagree, which is our right, we follow our own autonomous conscience without any consequence. If the Church presumes to correct us, we can dissent or leave. This is not an expression of the Catholic teaching that conscience must be obeyed; rather, it is the theory that conscience cannot err.

Together, *liberalism* and *Protestantism* are the political and religious names that we give to the same moral anthropology — a moral anthropology that is, at best, in tension with Catholic discipleship, and at worst is contrary to and incompatible with it. It is based in individual rights, voluntarism, and privatized morality.

And this is the faith of a very large number of American Catholics. Many of us American Catholics are liberals before we are Catholic. Thus we subscribe to and practice the moral and political language of liberalism as the foundation and structure of our religious, moral, and political lives. Specific Catholic moral teachings may fill some gaps, but these doctrines are subordinate, and thus answerable, to our own autonomous consciences. We have learned the language of liberalism while forgetting the language of Catholicism.

Learning a New Language and Forgetting the Old

Among my favorite novels is a series of books by the late British novelist Patrick O'Brian, popularly known as the Aubrey-Maturin novels. They follow the lives and careers of an early nineteenth-century British Navy captain, Jack Aubrey, and his best friend and erstwhile ship's surgeon, Stephen Maturin. The novels take Captain Aubrey and Dr. Maturin to the farthest reaches of the planet from England, and back again. In one of the novels, *The Nutmeg of Consolation*, Aubrey and Maturin lay in at the harbor of a small, fictional Melanesian Island called Sweeting's Island.[1] There, they discovered that the entire population, save two young girls about ages five and six, had died from a smallpox epidemic, probably brought to the island by British or American whalers.

When Dr. Maturin discovered the girls, they were near starvation, and barely spoke. As O'Brian describes the initial discovery, the girls' "minds were stunned not so much by terror or grief but more by utter bewilderment and incomprehension."[2] They could not understand what had happened to them, nor who (or what) these white men were who had appeared from nowhere. After determining that there were no other survivors on the island, Dr. Maturin took the girls on board the ship, with the hope of placing them in a foster or adoption home in New South Wales on the way home or, failing that, upon return to England. Dr. Maturin named the girls Emily and Sarah.

To communicate with the girls, the ship's company began to teach them English, the progress of which was "extraordinarily rapid."[3] Within a short time the girls "already [spoke] with a broad West-Country burr on the forecastle and in quite another English dialect on the quarterdeck."[4] Indeed, so impressive and rapid was their ability to speak these dialects of English, Captain Aubrey surmised, "It seems to me that they are forgetting their own language. You never hear them hallooing to one another in foreign as they used." This led another officer to wonder, "Could you ever forget your own language? Languages you have learnt, like Latin and Greek, yes; but your own?"[5] O'Brian does not provide an answer in the form of further dialogue, but rather through the narrator's description of Dr. Maturin's own linguistic journey: "At one time he had nearly forgotten his native Irish, the first language he ever spoke, [having been fostered] in the County Clare; and although it had surged up from the depths these last years when he spoke it ... there were still words, and quite commonplace ones too, whose sounds were perfectly familiar but whose meaning escaped him entirely."[6]

Finding Sarah and Emily a home in New South Wales failed, so they were taken to England. By the time they had arrived, as described in a subsequent novel, *The Commodore*, Emily and Sarah "had entirely forgotten the language of Sweeting's Island, apart from counting in it as they skipped, but they spoke perfect English, quarterdeck with never an oath or the much more earthy and emphatic lower-deck version, as occasion required."[7] That is, they had learned two dialects of English: the proper and formal language of the officers' deck and the saltier dialect of the enlisted seamen. But in the process, Emily and Sarah had forgotten their native language, except the rote recitation of numbers that accompanied their skipping. They no longer spoke, thought in, or presumably even understood their native tongue. Their language had been reduced to two dialects of the ambient language of a nineteenth-century British man-of-war.

I feel a little like Emily and Sarah when they first boarded the ship. In attempting to outline this book, I found myself struggling "not so much by terror or grief but more by utter bewilderment and incomprehension." For example, I wanted to write a book to help American Catholics ground our moral reasoning, especially on public issues, in a vision of Catholic social doctrine rather than individual rights. This implies situating our moral thought in the four pillars of the Church's social doctrine: dignity, the common good, subsidiarity, and solidarity. This is bewildering enough, because it is not at all clear that I can even define these phrases in a way that will be comprehensible to most American Catholics. Nor is it clear to me that this is a failure of my own abilities — modest as they assuredly are — but rather a broader and perhaps intractable problem even for those much more capable than myself. This reminded me of a famous thought experiment in Alasdair MacIntyre's groundbreaking 1981 book, *After Virtue*. MacIntyre asks us to imagine that the public blames the natural sciences for a series of environmental disasters. In reaction, laboratories are burned down, physicists are murdered, and scientific books and instruments are destroyed. Eventually, teaching of science in schools and universities is outlawed.

After a period of time, a new enlightened class comes to power and attempts to restore the natural sciences to their prior place of prominence:

> But all that they possess are fragments: a knowledge of experiments detached from any knowledge of the theoretical context which gave them significance; parts of theories unrelated either to the other bits and pieces of theory which they possess or to experiment; instruments whose use has been forgotten; half-chapters from books, single pages from articles, not always fully legible because torn and charred. Nonetheless all these fragments are reembodied in a set of practices which go under the revived names of physics, chemistry, and biology. Adults argue with each other about the respective merits of relativity theory, evolutionary theory, and phlogiston theory, although they possess only a very partial knowledge of each. Children learn by heart the

surviving portions of the periodic table and recite as in-
cantations some of the theorems of Euclid. Nobody, or
almost nobody, realizes that what they are doing is not
natural science in any proper sense at all. For everything
that they do and say conforms to certain canons of consistency and coherence and those contexts which would
be needed to make sense of what they are doing have
been lost, perhaps irretrievably.[8]

Thus, "what would appear to be rival and competing premises
for which no further argument could be given would abound."[9]
Summarizing the point of the thought experiment, MacIntyre
says, "The hypothesis which I wish to advance is that in the actual world which we inhabit the language of morality is in the
same state of grave disorder as the language of natural science in
the imaginary world I have described."[10]

I believe that forty-odd years of moral and political regress
have proven MacIntyre's hypothesis correct. As such, in my "bewilderment and incomprehension," I am not even able to offer
definitions of *dignity, subsidiarity, solidarity,* and *common good*
with any confidence that the definitions will be understood by
my fellow Catholics, much less the broader culture. But I can
try to explain *why* we have no common language — defined by
the necessary moral contexts and connotations. And I can make
tentative, but positive, suggestions about how we can overcome
this difficulty and learn to speak coherently to one another.

The problem MacIntyre describes can be called the "incommensurability thesis." The variety of moral languages (or frag-
ments thereof) spoken by disparate groups of people are rooted
in stories and contexts that assume widely different and largely incompatible views of the world. Thus two people may use
a common term (*justice*, for example) and mean very different
things by it — indeed, so different that justice for one person

might be abjectly unjust to another. This is because the relative narrative contexts — the stories — that give the words meaning for each speaker are incommensurate with one another. What makes the difficulty even more daunting is that we Catholics often use moral terms and phrases that are formed by these incommensurate stories, without even being aware that we are doing so.

There are two broad implications of the incommensurability thesis that make the project of recovering a common moral language a daunting task: (1) We are often unable to communicate with one another, and (2) we are unable to judge one moral assertion (or set of assertions) in terms of another. For example, two people may be passionate advocates for respecting the dignity of human persons, believing that this is a core moral value that must always be respected. But for one of the two, this necessarily implies that persons with severe disabilities, illness, disease, or just old age should have the liberty to take their own lives (or ask others legally to take their lives). For the other, dignity implies precisely the opposite: No person should take her own life, and the law should certainly not encourage or support another in taking it. The first advocate may be speaking within a moral framework that views individual personal autonomy as the highest good. The moral story for the second is that only God may take human life, and that dignity compels us to protect it from conception to natural death. How do we judge one in terms of the other?

More importantly, what if a Catholic, who *should* agree with the second advocate, actually thinks that the first advocate has it right? Yes, incommensurability is a problem when Catholics try to speak to non-Catholics, but my contention is more troubling than that. MacIntyre's thought experiment suggests that we Catholics cannot communicate with one another, because our moral languages are informed by a variety of incompatible

moral narratives, often rendering our conclusions morally inco-
herent or even unintelligible. Or, to the extent that we could be
said to have a common moral language, it is actually one that is
corrosive of robust Catholic public and political witness.

Even in this context of moral and political linguistic incommensurability, we still use certain moral terms by rote, often
without knowing what they mean. For example, as noted above,
modern liberal moral thought is dominated by a language of
"rights" that virtually all Americans, including American Catholics, uncritically embrace. But this language is the product of a
turn in moral philosophy away from the Catholic understanding
of the social nature of the human person to autonomous individualism. So, when we Catholics use it, are we embracing that
contradictory moral theory? Or are we using a language that we
do not really understand, but that undermines our deeper theological commitments? Put another way, are our moral languages
so overdetermined by rival moral theories that we do not even
have the language to account for that overdetermination? I believe the answer is yes.

What happened to Sarah and Emily is what has happened to
us Catholics in the United States today. We have learned to speak
the language of liberal Protestantism (either the Democratic or
Republican dialects), but other than rote words and phrases, we
have forgotten how to speak, or even think, Catholic. If we speak
Catholic, we are not understood in the public square; if we speak
the language of the public square, we are not speaking Catholic. In our attempt to be coherent or relevant, we may use the
same words, but we tend to modify their meaning so that they
are understood and accepted by the broader culture. Such moral
terms as *liberty, autonomy, agency, dignity, right, duty, justice,* or
voluntary are examples. If we use these terms the way American
secular culture uses them, we are not "speaking Catholic," even
though we think that we are. Our language has been reduced to

the two dialects of the liberal Protestantism that is spoken both on the quarterdeck and below decks. This makes it very difficult for us to speak coherently about Catholic moral doctrine, especially that branch that we call "social doctrine."

Why the Common Good Is Neither "Common" nor "Good"

One can see what I mean merely by comparing the doctrines of liberal Protestantism with the orthodoxy of secular liberalism. The former has been collapsed into the latter. For example, whether we call it liberal Protestantism or secular liberalism, it has its own definition of freedom. And it has either rejected the common good as mere code for authoritarianism or redefined it in such a way that it is neither common nor good.

Catholicism understands freedom in its full sense to be something that is achieved through moral choices ordered toward the good. Freedom cannot be reduced merely to our ability to choose among a variety of objects without regard to their moral content. Granted, the ability to choose between contrary options is necessary to call a human action a moral one. Without choice (or where the "choice" is coerced), an action is not, properly speaking, a moral action. We only ascribe morality to actions that are chosen free of constraint. Still, this is only the *necessary* condition for moral action; it is not the *sufficient* condition for a good moral action. For an action to have moral content — to be open to moral judgment — the person committing the action must be free from constraint or coercion in choosing the action. It is *necessary*, in other words, that a properly moral action be freely chosen.

But from the traditional Catholic Christian understanding, the mere absence of restraint (freedom to act) does not define the action as a *good* moral action. Rather, a good moral action is one that conforms with the proper end of the human person.

Contrast this with secular liberalism's "right to choose," for example. In this view, all that matters for the action to be morally good is that a radically autonomous individual makes it. There can be no judgment about *what* is chosen, but only *whether* it was the unfettered choice of the moral actor. In secular morality (descended from liberal Protestantism) freedom is both the necessary condition for a moral action and — because the only measure of good is the radical autonomy of the choice — it is the sufficient condition for a moral action to be "good."

This, again, is not the Catholic Christian understanding of a good moral action. As Saint Augustine puts it, "Free choice is sufficient for evil, but hardly for good."[11] Rather, because Catholics understand that good precedes choice, authentic human liberty is accomplished only when *the good* is freely chosen. As Pope St. John Paul II put it in a 1995 homily in Baltimore (appropriately enough): "Every generation of Americans needs to know that freedom consists not in doing what we like, but in having the right to do what we ought."[12]

Now contrast this with the typical liberal (sometimes called *libertarian*) understanding of freedom, which is commonly reduced to the ability to make the contrary choice. A "good" moral action is an action that is chosen free from constraints, without regard to the content of the action. In turn, freedom, in the language of one of the sixteenth-century founders of this theory, Thomas Hobbes, is "the absence of external impediments."[13] In this view, the right to make the individual choice among opposites is both the necessary *and* sufficient condition of the good, and thus of authentic human liberty. Indeed, any notion of a good that precedes, and therefore determines the propriety of, the choice is an inhibition of freedom. Under this notion, *good* is defined by the radically autonomous freedom to choose. Again, one hears the echo of this theory in phrases such as "free choice," "My body, my choice," and "pro-choice." This language is the natural heir of a theory that reduces the definition of *good* to "free from constraint."

This notion of freedom is summarized by the most funda-mental and all-encompassing moral term in American moral and political discourse: *subjective individual rights*. These rights, as Hobbes asserts, express "the liberty each man hath to use his own power as he will himself for the preservation of his own ... life; and consequently, of doing anything which, in his own judg-ment and reason, he shall conceive to be the aptest means there-unto."[14] This is the "natural right of every man to *every thing*."[15] According to this view of rights, every human being has a right to take everything he can, without regard to any prior claims of ownership by another.

Hobbes called this condition the "state of nature." For him and his intellectual heirs, radical individualism is the natural state of humankind. Community does not exist in the state of nature, and thus there are no external moral constraints against any person to do as he pleases. Rather, every person has a right to every thing. Because the human person is not naturally social, but radically individual, he has valid claims — natural rights — to do and to take what he wants if he has the means to do so. These rights have no *natural* limiting principle. "Nothing can be unjust"[16] in the state of nature, explains Hobbes. "The notions of right and wrong, justice and injustice, have there no place." Indeed, any notion of a natural limiting principle is already a de-nial of the fundamental nature of the right. It is no wonder, then, that Hobbes called this purported natural state of humankind a "war of every man against every man."[17]

Someone may object that the limiting principle is that one does not invade the rights of another person. This is not a prin-ciple, however, but rather a strategic agreement. It is a fictional contract between persons who mutually agree not to abridge one another's freedom. The only limit to my natural right to do as I please is the *conventional* agreement to limit the scope of the exercise of my rights for mutual consideration. As Hobbes explains it, when a person limits his rights, "it is ... in consideration of some right reciprocally transferred to himself."[18] This social contract, like all contracts, is a legal fiction, invented for the purpose of some semblance of political and legal predictability and, thus, safety. The important point, however, is that in this liberal theory, rights have no *natural* limits; their voluntary suspension is wholly an act of human convention. The contract is not transcended by any notion of the good, according to which one may not, for example, take the property of another or infringe the rights of another in pursuit of the exercise of one's own rights. Limiting my exercise of rights is not compelled due to some limiting notion of good, but rather merely to preserve my safety.[19]

This is the political, philosophical foundation of liberalism, the theory upon which the United States was built. And it is the moral and political language that we are uncritically taught from the beginnings of our education. Is it any wonder that we have forgotten a Catholic language of justice, the common good, solidarity, and charity?

The Right to Define Existence

Ultimately, this notion of individual rights implies more than every person having a claim upon the property of another. Rather, it implies that one has a right to define his or her very existence. Perhaps the paradigmatic example of how this notion of rights has shaped American legal and moral discourse is the famous "mystery" passage of U.S. Supreme Court Justice (and Catholic) Anthony Kennedy, in the 1992 case *Planned Parenthood of Southeastern Pennsylvania v. Casey*:

> Our law affords constitutional protection to personal

decisions relating to marriage, procreation, contraception, family relationships, child rearing, and education. Our cases recognize the right of the individual, married or single, to be free from unwarranted governmental intrusion into matters so fundamentally affecting a person as the decision whether to bear or beget a child. Our precedents have respected the private realm of family life which the state cannot enter. These matters, involving the most intimate and personal choices a person may make in a lifetime, choices central to personal dignity and autonomy, are central to the liberty protected by the Fourteenth Amendment. At the heart of liberty is the right to define one's own concept of existence, of meaning, of the universe, and of the mystery of human life.[20]

This gets us to the problem of how such officially articulated definitions of *freedom* and *individual rights* have necessary implications for a definition of *common good*. The notion of a common *good* (in contrast to disparate common *goods*) necessarily implies some given end toward which the human person is directed. Even though a society might define the common good solely in terms of a set of procedural conditions — individual rights, free speech, freedom of assembly, for example — the set of conditions is founded in, and established for the purpose of achieving, a substantive theory about the human person. Justice Kennedy would defend himself by saying that he is only describing the procedural space by which persons may define their own reality. But this necessarily implies a *substantive* understanding that the human person is radically autonomous and individual, and that society makes no morally legitimate claims upon him. This is one of the most important myths about a so-called procedural republic. It claims that it merely carves out a set of spaces and procedures in which the human person can pursue his own theory of the good. But this presupposes the *substantive* view that there is no proper end of moral action. The procedural space serves the substantive vision. And it is a vision that contradicts fundamental Catholic moral theology.

For example, the *Catechism of the Catholic Church* quoting the Second Vatican Council document *Gaudium et Spes*, defines the *common good* as "the sum total of social conditions which allow people, either as groups or as individuals, to reach their fulfillment more fully and more easily" (1906). As such, the common good consists of three elements: (1) respect for the person (see 1907); (2) the social development and well-being of the group itself (1908); and (3) peace, defined as "the stability and security of a just order" (1909). As a mirror image of Justice Kennedy's notion of common good, this definition presupposes substantive understandings of such terms as *person, well-being,* and *just order.* As the only creatures created in the image and likeness of God, humans are ordered toward God as our ultimate good. That foundation serves to define these other terms.

Yet if Justice Kennedy is correct about what is central to the rights implied by constitutional liberty, it is not merely difficult to talk about the common good, it is impossible. For this theory of rights and liberty is hostile to and corrosive of any truly Catholic notion of the common good. This idea of rights-based liberty necessarily rejects any concept of the proper end of common moral life. Indeed, the whole point of the theory is that there is no such thing as a common good. Thus each individual rights-bearing person is free to pursue his private view of the good. To the extent that the term *common good* still has any use in such a scheme, it is nothing more than the accumulation of individual goods attained by autonomous rights-bearers as they not only seek their own good, but define the good in the act of seeking it.

Moreover, in the Catholic tradition the worship of God is

rooted in fundamental justice. *Justice* is classically defined as giving to another his or her due. God, and God alone, is due our worship. We act justly, both individually and corporately, when we worship God. When our worship is directed to anyone or anything else, we commit an act of injustice toward God. Thus, in the Catholic understanding, the good that orders our lives is not the freedom to be able to worship God, but the actual worship of God. The common good is the sum of the conditions that make that not only possible, but facilitate it, allowing us to reach it "more fully and easily." In summary, the common good is (among other things) a particular, substantive set of conditions that facilitate the worship of God.

This contrasts starkly with the prevailing American concept of the common good in public life, which sees the "good" merely as clearing the public square so that different visions of the good can compete with one another in a moral game of survival of the fittest. Such a notion of good is not at all "common."

The problem is not just that non-Catholics believe in this concept of the common good. Rather, the moral anthropology suggested by Justice Kennedy is largely embraced even by a large number — if not a majority — of American Catholics. (And let us keep in mind that Justice Kennedy himself is a professed Catholic.) Justice Kennedy describes a view of the human person that has formed the American moral conscience. And it is the view that largely prevails across the religious and political spectrum in the United States. It is expressed, for example, when a Catholic "decides for himself" whether to follow the teaching of the Church on this or that issue. Contraception is the lowest of the low-hanging fruit, but, as I will argue throughout this book, this view infects other areas of moral deliberation, including issues related to family, work, economics, and politics. We might mock Kennedy's language, but we largely form our moral practices precisely as he describes it. And this is true regardless of whether we identify as conservative or liberal.

One reason that we have succumbed to Justice Kennedy's understanding of the liberty to define one's own existence is that we are formed by the moral and political narratives of American independence, individualism, and exceptionalism, often without any conscious realization that this is the case. The tradition of moral autonomy in modern liberalism tells us that we can stand apart from moral, cultural, and political influences to decide for ourselves from a position of moral independence and autonomy. But that belief is itself a product of a particular set of political narratives that make claims upon our moral reasoning. We are the pioneers, the rugged individualists, the libertarians, upon whom you shall not tread. Ayn Rand's *Atlas Shrugged* is the great American novel.

We Speak a Common Language of Liberalism with Partisan Accents

One of the difficulties in this discussion is our use of the terms *conservative* and *liberal* in defining what we usually mean by competing political visions. My definition of *liberal* encompasses both. And both sides tend to agree that the common good (if the phrase is used at all) is nothing more than the space created for the pursuit of discrete goods by individuals. But this is to define the common good away. Liberal attempts (whether of the right or left variety) to define the common good must define it such that it winds up being neither "common" nor (at least from a Catholic perspective) "good." Rather, it means the accumulation and measurement of disparate goods, each as defined by individual bearers of natural rights in a Hobbesian state of nature.

Now, in one sense, to invoke a famous image from Saint Augustine, every political society holds some ultimate good in common (although Augustine framed it more in terms of love than good). In explaining the Fall of Adam and Eve in *The Literal*

Meaning of Genesis, Augustine describes the two exclusive loves that animate human moral action: love of God or love of self. "One is holy, the other unclean; one turned towards the neighbor, the other centered on self," he observes; "one looking to the common good ... the other ... arrogantly looking to domination."[21] He expands the point in the most famous passage of his magisterial treatise of Christian political philosophy, *The City of God*, where he explains that the two exclusive objects of love form the two exclusive kinds of cities: "Two cities have been formed by two loves: the earthly by the love of self, even to the contempt of God; the heavenly by the love of God, even to the contempt of self. The former, in a word, glories in itself, the latter in the Lord."[22]

Properly ordered love is directed toward God, while disordered love is directed toward the self — "one subject to God, the other rivaling him."[23] Love of self is a usurpation of love, to the exclusion of love of God. Love of God necessarily includes proper love of self. This implies that when the city is properly ordered toward love of God, it will be properly ordered in every other way. If worship of God is the object of the love of the city, the city will otherwise properly order love among its citizens. In a passage that could have predicted Thomas Hobbes's "war of every man against every man" in the state of nature, Saint Augustine concludes that the city ordered toward love of self is "tempestuous" and "seditious," while the city ordered toward love of God is "tranquil" and "peaceful."[24]

It goes without saying that this is not a definition of love that would sit well with the ACLU. But it does present the general problem of the relationship between the religious believer and the secular state. And it goes to the problem of religious faith in the public square. On the one hand, these two competing visions of the city are mutually exclusive. On the other hand, the city is comprised of people who hold one of these two visions, including those who, however imperfectly, attempt to order their love toward God. How, then, do these two cities coexist? And how should we Catholic Christians understand the relationship?

Christians Are Citizens Everywhere and Strangers Everywhere

A second-century apologetic letter known as the *Epistle to Diognetus* is one of the earliest attempts to address the relationship of Christians to the state. This letter may suggest a way to think about, if not resolve, this problem. Written from an anonymous author to an unknown recipient, the epistle defends the religious, cultural, and political practices of the Church during a time of suspicion and persecution. And while the political climate of the second-century Roman Empire was significantly different from the twenty-first-century United States, the epistle offers guidance that is still relevant on the relationship of Christian faith and practice to political identity and allegiance. And it suggests a way of thinking about political practice that can help us to think more deeply about how partisan identification may lead to the erosion of authentic Christian witness.

In chapter 5 of the *Epistle to Diognetus*, the author explains, "Christians are indistinguishable from other men either by nationality, language or customs. They do not inhabit separate cities of their own, or speak a strange dialect, or follow some outlandish way of life." Instead, he continues, "With regard to dress, food and manner of life in general, they follow the customs of whatever city they happen to be living in, whether it is Greek or foreign."[25] Christianity is not defined in terms of any particular social, demographic, linguistic, or political community, so Christian faith and practice are not conditioned by these contingencies.

But perhaps more importantly, because Christianity is not defined by any of these contingencies, it also cannot be *identified* with any of them. Its independence from them necessarily implies its resistance to being reduced to them. Christians can live under a wide variety of cultural and political systems, but this entails resistance to identification with any cultural or political philosophies, narratives, and intellectual justifications. This includes identification with any particular political theory or unqualified allegiance to any particular regime. The epistle's author observes that while Christians are "obedient to the laws, *they yet live on a level that transcends the law*" (my emphasis).[26]

Now, of course, the epistle is an apologetic letter, written by a Christian to explain and defend Christian faith and practice. Its descriptions of second-century Christian life might be more aspirational than descriptive. Nonetheless, the observation that Christians live on a level that transcends the law is an important one, rich with meaning for the way that we might think about political identity and partisan loyalty. And it reflects a model for Christian citizenship that has largely been lost in American political culture. Christians may obey the law, and even engage in broader civic life, but the rationale for this participation is found not in the principles — or the languages — of the regime, but rather in a distinct Christian dialect. We are called to obey the laws of the regime. But we should not justify our obedience in terms of those laws, but rather in terms of the principles of the rich tradition of Christian moral doctrine. And those doctrines should not be reduced to political life or identified with any political party.

Because the justification for obedience to the laws of the regime is based in Christian theology and not the terms of the regime itself, Christians necessarily live in tension with the regime. We obey its laws (with exceptions that I discuss in chapter 7), but we resist justifying that obedience in its terms. More importantly, we resist justifying the law itself in the terms of our Christian faith. The laws of the regime, like any, may be supported by an admixture of just and unjust principles. But regardless of the relative morality of the foundation of those laws, Christians will not underwrite them by their own theological conviction. By this I mean that we do not search around for a way to justify the law of the regime in terms of our Christian faith.

Why? Because when we do so, we soon would find ourselves molding our theological convictions to support the moral foundations of these laws. Like Sarah and Emily from the O'Brian novels, this is how we forget the theological language that formed us in the first place, and which should be an alternative to the morality of the age. What begins as using Christian theology to justify politics ends up with Christians unable to distinguish between theological truth and political compromise. The regime will only be justified in its own terms and sustained by its own narratives. Thus for Christians to participate in that justification necessarily causes us to change the terms of our own story to fit those of the regime. Before long, the former is reduced to the latter, and authentic Christian witness is lost.

To use an example that will be prominent in the pages that follow, we Catholics join virtually all of our fellow countrymen in recognizing individual rights as a fundamental political category. Indeed, for Americans, political discourse is almost always framed in terms of individual, private rights. While Catholics certainly may observe and respect political or legal rights (so long as they do not force us directly to commit sin), we must be very cautious in the rationale we use to do so. For typical Americans, *political* rights are based upon liberal individual *moral* rights.

By political rights, I mean the legal privileges or protections that are created by laws or regulations, usually based upon some conditions. For example, if I meet all the requirements for obtaining a driver's license, and have no disqualifying conditions, I have a right to drive a car on public roadways without arbitrary restrictions. This right cannot be taken away from me for any reason other than failing to meet one of the conditions for obtaining it. Similarly, legal rights might take the form of licenses to use federal lands for grazing, state-owned lands for hunting, or public waters for fishing. These are rights that are created by legislation, regulation, or administrative directive. They are not rooted in nature, or in a theory of the human person.

While these political rights can be unproblematic, the language of individual moral rights is fraught with dangers. As I argue in chapter 3, individual moral rights are in tension (if not incompatible) with a Catholic understanding of the human person. Even when we justify a language of political or legal "rights," this justification is often rooted in a theory of individual moral rights that actually may be corrosive of Catholic witness.

When we do not simply obey the laws but feel compelled to justify them, the transcendent foundation of our civic friendship is forgotten, and our witness to the story of Christ is compromised. This is especially true when the prevailing political language tells us that we are natural enemies of one another, making competing claims of individual rights.

Toward a Theology of Civic Friendship

The *Catechism* defines the duties of citizens not primarily in political terms, but rather in broader terms of civic friendship (see 2239). This is based upon the uniquely Christian understanding of the human person and her place in, and relationship to, broader civic culture. "It is the *duty of citizens* to contribute along with the civil authorities to the good of society in a spirit of truth, justice, solidarity, and freedom," the *Catechism* explains. If we observe this duty, we will not think of ourselves primarily as political adversaries, with every policy question being a loser-takes-all zero-sum game. Rather, a theology of civic friendship suggests that we think primarily in terms of social goods that benefit us all. Civic friendship can be thought of as the antonym of political rivalry. But in the United States, we are more likely to think of ourselves as political rivals, rather than civic friends. And this rivalry commits us to one of two political parties, both of which hold positions that are inconsistent with — if not opposed to — Catholic moral theology. As Pope Francis has put it, "Genuine social friendship within a society makes true universal openness possible."[27]

This duty is both broader than mere political engagement, and at the same time delimiting of the role of politics in civic life. The good of society includes the full scope of social relationships, of which political participation is but one of many — and often the least important. As such, the mandate suggests that identifying ourselves by political party affiliation cannot be the sole, or even the primary, way that we fulfill our duty to contribute to civic life. Reducing civic friendship to political identification or activity tends to erode the former, as we are forced to pick sides. Thus we descend from civic friendship to political identification to party loyalty, and our theological commitments erode from principles that transcend political parties to ideologies that underwrite them.

This problem is at least implicitly raised by John Courtney Murray, SJ, in a famous passage from his book *We Hold These Truths*. "The question is sometimes raised, whether Catholicism is compatible with American democracy," he observes. "The question is invalid as well as impertinent; for the manner of its position inverts the order of values," he continues. "It must, of course, be turned round to read, whether American democracy is compatible with Catholicism."[28]

A pluralist, democratic society requires "agreement and consensus" in order to function, which raises "no small political problem," Murray dryly observes. "How is it that this common assent and consent do not infringe upon the 'freedom of religion,' that is, the freedom of consciences to retain the full integrity of their own convictions, and the freedom of the churches to maintain their own different identities, as defined by themselves. ... To resign this freedom or to abdicate this right would be at once the betrayal of religion and the corruption of politics."[29] And, cutting to the bone, he asserts, "The Catholic may not, as others do, merge his religious and his patriotic faith, or submerge one in the other."[30]

While he does not expressly invoke the notion of competing moral or political languages, as I have in this chapter, Murray nonetheless alludes to the problem. The Catholic "must reckon with his own tradition of thought, which is wider and deeper than any that America has elaborated." But the Catholic also "must recognize that a new problem has been put to the universal Church by the American doctrine and project in the matter of pluralism." By pluralism, Murray does not mean a melting pot of ethnicities, languages, and demographic characteristics. Rather, he is talking about the very problem of incommensurability that I discussed earlier in this chapter. Murray notes that the "conceptual equipment for dealing with the problem is by no means lacking to the Catholic intelligence."[31] But I am not confident that American Catholics today have faithfully maintained that conceptual equipment; rather, we have allowed it to be merged with moral and political language that is foreign to the actual teachings of the Church. Rather than developing a "catholic" language to deal with the problem of pluralism, we have succumbed to the pluralism itself. Rather than a problem to be addressed, it has become a good to be embraced. This, of course, is consistent with the radical individualism exemplified by Justice Kennedy.

This is especially important when we consider partisan identity. It is a mistake to justify one's partisan identification by theological argument, but we go even further when we attempt *partisan* justification of our *theological* commitments. This collapses the latter into the former and verges (at best) on idolatry.

For example, when "conservative" Catholics express opinions about, say, immigration, their moral commitments are usually more formed by Republican Party politics than the Catholic doctrine of solidarity of all mankind. Similarly, when "liberal" Catholics talk about abortion, they are usually aping the Democratic Party platform, rather than the Catholic doctrine of the image of God. The result is that we compromise the integrity of our theological commitments, and these commitments no longer transcend our political and partisan loyalties. Instead, our partisan loyalties determine our moral commitments, and we pay obeisance accordingly. To put it in Father Murray's terms, we forget the "conceptual equipment" for dealing with the problem.

This is not to suggest that Catholics withdraw from political life. To resist partisan identification is not to abdicate our civic responsibly. But we should be more cautious about two tendencies: first, to reduce the mandate for civic friendship to one for political activity, and second, to reduce political activity to partisan loyalty. We should also reaffirm the principle of subsidiarity in the way that we think about civic life and political action. Subsidiarity, which I discuss in detail in chapter 3, is the aspect of Catholic social doctrine demanding that social challenges and needs be met at the smallest and most local level possible. Main Street should have a more immediate purchase on our civic lives than Pennsylvania Avenue; and the St. Vincent de Paul Society's purchase is more immediate still. If we Christians were to live our civic lives as though politics mattered less, we might find that — well, politics matters less. And we would thus be more likely to resist the siren call of the kind of partisan zealotry that defeats civic friendship.

I am well aware that this raises a difficult objection: It leaves politically engaged Catholics in the partisan wilderness. But this may well be part of the cost of faithful Christian discipleship. For example, while both major parties in the United States today assert that they are committed to abstract moral terms like *dignity*, neither party can be taken seriously in those claims. One party talks about the dignity of the unborn and (perhaps) the elderly and ill, but minimizes (and effectively denies) the dignity of the immigrant, the refugee, the prisoner, or those persons unable to participate in the market. The other party might affirm the dignity of the immigrant, but denies it for the unborn or aged. It is not our role to try to save these political parties from themselves.

But here is the essence of the problem: Because most Catholics subscribe to the definition given them by their partisan identification, we have not maintained the moral language or the moral skill to explain why both sides are wrong. We Catholics tend to identify first as Democrats or Republicans, and then mold our "Christian" moral vocabulary to their respective platforms. Or, worse, like Emily and Sarah, we have completely forgotten the moral language of the Church, having learned one or the other dialect of American liberal politics.

In his book *A Community of Character*, theologian Stanley Hauerwas suggests that this has resulted in Christians "hav[ing] failed to challenge the moral presuppositions of our polity and society. ... The more destructive result is that the church has increasingly imitated in its own social life the politics of liberalism."[32] This is evident in all sorts of observable ways. For example, during the pandemic, many Catholics framed resistance to social distancing and even limited attendance at Mass and other liturgies in terms of our "individual rights" to gather where and when we please. This completely disregarded principles of solidarity or the common good. These impulsive moral gestures are formed by the language of liberalism rather than that of the Church.

And when we think like this, we not only get our moral language from liberalism; in turn we justify liberalism in terms of our supposed Christian faith, thus subordinating the latter to the former. Because we have already accepted the dialect — and forgotten our own language — we do not have the moral vocabulary to object to a polity that is the inevitable result of the moral language. By accepting the liberal Protestant privatizing of morality, we stand mute when morality is privatized. As Hauerwas puts it, "It was assumed that in making 'morality' a matter of the 'private sphere' — that is, what we do with our freedom — it could still be sustained and have a public impact."[33] But this failed to take account of the necessity that the morality to which, for example, the founders referred, must be sustained through a continuity of language, or else it will be forgotten.

In the chapters that follow, I outline the possibility of recovering a spiritual and moral language, rooted in and consistent with the Catholic understanding of the human person. I apply that moral language, through the rich history of Catholic social doctrine, to some perennial categories of public issues: family, work, economic life, and political life. Finally, I suggest the practice of charitable conversation through civic friendship as a possible practical way to implement my suggestions. This is based on thinking about Alasdair MacIntyre's famous conclusion in *After Virtue* that we may be waiting for a new Saint Benedict. I suggest in the concluding chapter to this book that the best way to think about this is not through retreat, but rather through a language and posture of civic friendship, rooted in charity. This is a *community* of civic friendship based upon the *communication* of Christian charity.

Chapter 2

Creation, Fall, and Alienation: How We Forgot That We Are Social Beings

In chapter 1, I used a quote from U.S. Supreme Court Justice Anthony Kennedy as a proxy for a prominent, widely accepted theory about the nature of the human person. Our understanding of what it means to be human — what we are in the essence of our being, how we shape our moral lives, how we teach ourselves to act — is the beginning of all moral and political discussions. Because all social institutions will both flow from and reinforce what we think of ourselves, we cannot think about moral, political, or social issues without considering what we are as human beings. The nature of the human person is the starting point for all questions of public life.

To reach a proper understanding of the nature of the human person (and how that nature has been compromised), we must begin at the beginning. Catholic Christians understand that those questions are addressed in the very beginning of the Jewish and Christian Revelation, in the Book of Genesis. Throughout this book, I will make many references to the biblical accounts of creation and the Fall in the Book of Genesis. Through the deeply symbolic structure and language of Genesis, we can begin to see how the human person is created as a social creature, how we have rejected the truth of that nature, and how that rejection has affected the way we form our moral, spiritual, and political lives. As we will see, Genesis presents us with a very different understanding of the human person than that of Justice Kennedy and those who subscribe to his notion that we create our own reality.

Reading as a Moral and Social Task

Before we look carefully at these early chapters of the Bible, let's consider some principles that we should apply in reading a text — any text, not just the Bible. As noted in chapter 1, our moral and spiritual lives are often formed by narratives and stories of which we are not even aware. In America, these stories are variations on liberal individualism, which impacts how we approach a text, especially the Bible. Reading a text is itself an aspect of moral practice. To the extent that it is possible, we must allow a text to speak to us on its own terms, as determined by the meaning and purposes of its author (or authors). This is not an easy task, especially when we are reading ancient texts or texts that do not readily yield a clear, unambiguous meaning. But regardless of the difficulty in properly reading and interpreting a text, we can apply certain principles to guide us. These principles will help us to allow a text to speak for itself (to the degree possible) and will stop us from imposing a meaning upon the text that its author did not intend.

I am not denying that a text is capable of yielding more than one meaning, or that some texts may support multiple reasonable interpretations or applications. Sometimes a text may yield different but complementary interpretations. There may be truths to be found there that are compatible with the author's intention, but which she did not (or perhaps could not) expressly envision. Other times, they may yield rival incompatible interpretations, both (or several) of which are reasonable. Nor do my suggestions for approaching a text ignore the problem of our own contextualization, which will have constraining effects on the way we read.

In other words, we are a product of various narrative structures — some true, some false, many mixed with both — that shape even the way we read a book or listen to a song. As I suggested in chapter 1, in the United States, stories and myths of autonomy, individualism, self-expression, and self-reliance are the primary narratives that shape our lives. We can try to identify the stories that claim our moral lives, but we can never completely stand outside them, as though there is some privileged point of view immune from all contingencies. But in every case, we must try to allow the text to speak for itself, in its own style, voice, tone, and form, rather than to impose our own expectation upon it. All of which is to say that reading is hard work. And it is a moral exercise, demanding that we apply the same virtues that ought to attend other aspects of our lives.

In her book *Reading for the Love of God*, Jessica Hooten Wilson, the Fletcher Jones Endowed Chair of Great Books at Pepperdine University, has described two errors to avoid when we approach a text, and then a middle way by which we can avoid both errors. The errors consist of either imposing the meaning upon a text, on the one hand, or assuming that a text is immune from the contingencies and contexts that claim both the author and the reader, on the other hand.

The first error is to approach the text as though it has no meaning at all other than what the reader imposes upon it.[1] For theorists of this way of reading, it is not only wrong to think that the text can speak for itself, but also futile. There is no meaning other than that which the reader brings to it from his own subjective experiences. Of course, a corollary to this is that all reading is an idiosyncratic exercise by each reader, by which no judgment can be made about whether a text is read correctly or incorrectly. Indeed, the "correct" reading for one reader may be fundamentally contradicted by the "correct" reading of another. Neither may judge the veracity or accuracy of the other, because the text itself is not an objective reference to which we may point. The subjective experience and reaction of the reader is the "meaning." Wilson acknowledges that questions about the subjective effects of reading are not invalid. Indeed, what the text "does" is often as important as what it says. But they are not the only or even the primary questions.[2]

The second error that Wilson describes is to assume that a text is nothing other than an object to be critically examined, but which is not read for the truth claims that it might be making.[3] In this way of reading, we reduce texts to an expression of the prejudices of the community that formed the authors who composed them. Thus we read a text not for its meaning, but rather for the political, moral, or social culture in which it is embedded and from which it cannot be extracted. In contrast to the first error described above, the meaning is not determined by the reader, but rather by the social pathologies that produced the text. The text is nothing more than an expression of its social milieu. Discover that milieu and we discover the real meaning of the text. In contemporary literary theory, this is almost always expressed in terms of structures of oppression. The intention of the author is irrelevant because he was not free from the biases or chauvinism that dictated his text.

To be clear, elements of both of these erroneous approaches to reading a text are sometimes legitimate considerations. For example, the experiences of a reader or group of readers may tease out truths from a text that its author did not — or in some cases could not — envision. But when this occurs, we do not say that it is true for one person, but false for another. As to the second error in approaching the text, we cannot deny the moral, social, and political contexts in which an author wrote, nor the constraining influences of those contexts. But we do not conclude from this that the text is solely the product of these environments, entirely muting the voice of the author. In both cases, the error is not in acknowledging these legitimate elements, but rather in reducing the text to nothing other than what the reader imposes upon it, on the one hand, or the cultural constraints of the author on the other.

The better approach, suggests Wilson, is to take seriously all three elements of a text: "the author, the reader, and the text" itself.[4] All three considerations are necessary aspects of trying to find the truth of a text. Sometimes that truth will be expressly intended by the author; other times it will be a necessary (but unforeseen) corollary; in still others, the truth will only emerge in the context of future contingencies. The point is, though, that we take seriously the notion that the text is trying to convey some truth claims, and that those truth claims are not simply the product of the author's environment or the reader's subjective experience.

With this in mind, and before we turn to the text of Genesis, let us consider the *kinds* of meaning that an author or text can make. Historically, beginning at least with Saint Augustine, theologians have identified four different kinds of meaning (four "senses") that we can find in Scripture. "In all the sacred books," wrote Augustine, "we should consider the eternal truths that are taught, the facts that are narrated, the future events that are predicted, and the precepts or counsels that are given."[5] Today, this list has been refined thus:

- The "literal" sense (Augustine's "facts that are narrated")
- The "anagogical" sense (roughly Augustine's "future events")
- The "allegorical" sense (roughly Augustine's "eternal truths")
- The "moral" sense (Augustine's "precepts or counsels")

These four senses (the literal and three spiritual senses) have a venerable tradition in the Church, and they continue to have important uses. But I am concerned that the structure of these four senses can be distracting. This is especially true when we deal with the idea of "literal" truth. Our minds have largely been trained to divide claims simply into "literally true" and "not true." And the "literal truth" is reduced to what can be measured by a clock or calendar — some event that took place in quantifiable space and time. If a claim or story cannot meet this rigid criterion, it cannot be "literal" truth. I want to suggest instead that any claim of truth is a claim of *literal* truth. To be sure, literal truth may be conveyed in many kinds of literature. But when an author makes a claim of truth, whether through poetry, fable, legend, song, or historical narrative, he wants us to believe that the claim is *literally* true. This is crucial for reading Genesis.

When we turn to the first chapters of Genesis, we often doom a good reading by asking the inappropriate question of whether the creation account in Genesis 1 is "literal" — in other words, does it account for six chronological days of creation. For many readers, the literal truth of Genesis (and thus its legitimacy) stands or falls upon the answer to that question. This approach to Genesis insists that it is making claims that can be judged by tools of history and science. This is an attempt to reconcile Genesis 1 with what we know (or think we know) about things like the age of the earth. When we do this, we force the creation account in Genesis 1 to make claims that its author did not intend.

The question, then, is not whether a truth is literal. All truth is literal truth. And every time an author makes a claim of truth, he wants it to be taken as literal truth, whether about morality, psychology, theology, or social reality. Rather, there are two questions that should be asked. First, how are the truth claims being conveyed? (Or what kind of literature is being utilized to make the claim?) Second, how are these truth claims to be interpreted?[6]

In approaching the Bible, we must be attentive to the literary form we are reading so that we can properly interpret the literal truth that the author is attempting to convey (or the truth claim that he is making). If we impose our own expectation of what literary form is used, we risk missing both the claim being made and the truth it conveys. This is most especially true when we read the first chapters of Genesis.

The Poetry of Creation

Let us turn, then, to the first creation account (see Gn 1:1—2:3), asking ourselves what kind of literature we are reading. This question must be answered before we can ask what truth claim the author is making, as the truth claim cannot be separated from the literary genre.

Our first clue is found in the repetitive structure of Genesis 1. Six times a passage begins "Then God said ..." and ends "Evening came, and morning followed."[7] The repetition reminds us of poetic verses or musical choruses. The lyrical quality of the verses lends itself to understanding their substance: We are reading poetry or a prose-poem. This is not incidental to the meaning and purpose of the first creation account. The poetic structure of chapter 1 gives us important clues about what kind of literature we are — and are not — reading. That kind of literature is poetic, or perhaps even musical.

The verses in Genesis 1 are making some kind of claim about creation. But what is that claim? If we consider the words between the framing set forth above, we get further clues. The six days of creation are structured in corresponding pairs. The first day corresponds to the fourth; the second to the fifth; the third to the sixth. Thus day and night correspond to sun and moon; sky and water to birds and fish; land and plants to animals of the earth (including humans). The sixth day is different from the first five, as it creates two qualitatively different kinds of things. On the sixth day, God first creates all the animals that are not human (see Gn 1:24–25). But then "God said: 'Let us make human beings in our image, after our likeness. … God created man in his image; in the image of God he created them; male and female he created them" (Gn 1:26–27). Clearly the human creature is distinct from all other creatures, meriting special mention on the sixth day. (In my discussion of the family in chapter 4, I will discuss verse 27 in more detail, especially the account of the human person being created as "male and female.") But, while the passage is longer, the sixth day still holds to the pattern; and it still corresponds to the third day as noted above. Moreover, it clearly sets the human person apart as the creature to whom (and for whom) all other creation is ordered. The human creature has "dominion" over all the other animals and fish (Gn 1:28); and the seed-bearing plants (from day three) are created as his food (1:29).[8]

This poetic ordering tells us that we are not reading a scientific account of creation. Our author is not interested in telling us how or when the universe came into being. Rather, both by the literary form and the orderly content of the prose-poem, the author is making the claim that the universe is orderly. Some things are ordered toward and by other things. The "truth" of the six days of creation has nothing to do with the origins or the age of the universe, but rather with the natural ordering and purpose of creation. From the form and content of the account, we can reasonably surmise that the author of Genesis is suggesting that creation has a poetic structure and order. We might even say that the universe is itself the poem, spoken by God and recorded by the sacred author. This is the *literal* meaning of creation. As spoken into creation by God, it is poetic and orderly.

Finally, of course, the first creation account ends with a seventh day. But this day is different from the other six in two important ways. First, it does not begin with the words "Then God said," followed by some act of creation. No work of creation occurs on the seventh day at all, in fact. It just "is." God is finished with the work he has been doing, so he rests on and blesses the seventh day. This implies that the seventh day may be identified with God himself. This suggestion is supported by the second important difference from the first six days: The seventh day does not have a different single day to which it is paired. Instead, all six of the days of creation are ordered toward the seventh. The seventh day is the day of rest in God; or even, we might suggest, the seventh day *is* rest in God. It is the day toward which all the work of creation is oriented.

This account of creation gives us the very foundation of the cause and purpose of our moral lives. It provides an account of the *end* and *purpose* toward which all creation is ordered. Creation (including the crown of creation, the human person) is *properly* ordered when — and only when — it is oriented toward God. Theologians call this idea *teleology*, from the Greek word *telos*, which means "end," "goal," or "purpose." Catholic moral theology is wholly built upon this foundation: that all creation is ordered toward its final purpose of rest (Sabbath) in God. Our moral lives are to be lived in such a way that they are consistent with that purpose. "This is not the expression of an otherworldly piety," explains Fr. Joseph Ratzinger (later Pope Benedict XVI), "but a clear and sober translation of the creation account and of the message that it bears for our lives."[9]

Catholic moral theology does not begin with lists of commands about what we may or may not do. It is not comprised merely of proscriptions and prescriptions. Rather, moral theology begins with the very structure of creation as ordered toward God. This is a positive approach to our moral life that does not see it as a drudgery of commands to be kept, but as the joy of orientation toward our proper purpose and end. Catholic moral theology begins with an understanding of who we are in the perfection of creation. We are beings to whom and for whom all creation is ordered; and in turn we are ordered toward Sabbath rest in God. We are ordered toward peace with God, the first creation account teaches us, in a world that is otherwise ordered toward us. This notion is more fully articulated in the second creation account from Genesis 2.

The Human Person and Community

A second way of describing creation is contained in most of the second chapter of Genesis (see vv. 4–25). Like the first, the second account is not interested in the age and origin of the universe, but rather in describing some truths about it. This account uses different images and symbols from the first to tell a different story about creation. Of course, its "literal" truth claims are complementary with the first. But these truth claims are made in a different literary style for the purpose of giving us more information about creation, humanity, and God. More specifically, the purpose of Genesis 2 is to describe the natural harmony of the human community with itself and with God. It does this by describing the extravagance of God's gifts to us.

The second creation account introduces us to the Garden of Eden, that primordial paradise, in which the humans are in harmony with one another and with God. After creating the first human being, God planted a garden for him that provided both physical and spiritual nourishment. The trees of the garden were not only "good for food," but also "delightful to look at" (Gn 2:9). By joining these two, the author is suggesting that the human is sustained not only by physical goods, but also moral goods, of which contemplation of beauty is an essential aspect. As in the first creation account, we have clues in the second that the moral life is not about restrictions but rather about positive goods that both sustain the human person and give him pleasure. Catholic moral theology is built upon yes, not no.

This is most acutely illustrated in God's instruction to the first human in the garden. This instruction is almost universally described in popular culture as one of restriction: God tells the human what he cannot do, namely, eat from one particular tree in the garden. But this is surely the wrong way to read Genesis 2. After describing the nourishment and beauty of the trees of the garden, God does not place narrow strictures on the man. Quite the opposite, God tells the man that he may enjoy an extravagance of goods, including, "You are free to eat from any of the trees of the garden" (Gn 2:16b). The presumption is one of generous permission to enjoy the rich variety of God's good creation. God liberally shares his creation with the human person. We are guests in God's garden. But we are guests who have been told, "Make yourselves completely at home."

Only after this expansive consent to enjoy all the trees does God issue one exception: the tree of knowledge of good and evil. "From that tree you shall not eat," God says; "when you eat from it you shall die" (Gn 2:17). But what does the restriction mean? What is that tree anyway? If God did not want us to eat from the tree of knowledge of good and evil, why put it in the garden at all? The answers to these questions take us deeper into some key foundational points about Catholic moral theology in general and particularly in our own moral lives.

The persistent foundational theme of both creation accounts is that God is Creator, not us. Therefore, we are participants in God's creation, not its originators. Even to the extent that we may "know," our knowing is a participation in the very mind of God, which, of course, precedes creation. God's mind — like God himself — is eternal. God shares his knowledge with us, and apart from his knowledge there is no human knowledge. And the knowledge we do have is incomplete and fragmentary. As creatures, we are naturally constrained by the contingencies of our own historical, temporal, and cultural conditions.

To put it simply, we are not the sources of intelligence, knowledge, meaning, and truth. To the extent we "possess" any of these faculties, it is only by our sharing in the mind of God. For example, we "possess" the knowledge that twice two equals four. But "twice two equals four" is not true because we "know" it, or because we have simply decreed it. Rather, we know it because it is true. And it is true only because it is part of the very intelligence that is the mind of God. We might assert that we are the sources of mathematical truth, and we hereby declare that twice two equals five. But, of course, every time we take two marbles and add them to two other marbles, we will have four marbles, not five.

Like mathematics, moral truths are immutable because they exist in the immutable mind of God. We do not originate them, we cannot change them, and believing something false about them does not make them so. We can reason from them, but we do not create them. Nor, of course, can we change them. To presume (or attempt) to do so is to participate in evil.

Beginning at least with Saint Augustine, Christian theologians have defined evil as the "privation of good." All things that exist are good because they are either God (perfect, incorruptible good) or are created by God (participant, corruptible good). God, who is all good, is not corruptible; there is no "thing" from which he can fall short. But created things are corruptible. They may be used in a way that is not ordered toward their proper goodness. When that which is created falls short of, or is disordered from, its created purpose, it is divested of its goodness. As Augustine put it in *Confessions*, "everything that is corrupted is deprived of some good."[10] Evil does not have its own being. It "has no positive nature," Augustine explains in *The City of God*. Rather, "the loss of good has received the name 'evil.'"[11]

This is the symbolism of the tree of the knowledge of good and evil. It is the explanation to the human person that good is given in nature as an expression of God's own nature. But it also tells us that it is possible for the human to use his freedom to choose against good, or to make choices that fall short of good. This gets us to what God means by telling the human that he may not eat of the tree of knowledge of good and evil. Among other possibilities, the tree represents the fact that all knowledge is in and from God. Apart from God there is no knowledge. By casting it in terms of "good and evil," God is telling us that all assertions of knowledge are either participations in his own eternal mind and good, or assertions that knowledge originates with us and thus is a corruption from good, or "evil."

From this we can see that God's direction not to eat from the tree of knowledge of good and evil is not so much about *permission*, as it is about *possibility*. It is not so much "You are not allowed to eat" from the tree as it is "You are not able to eat" from the tree. It is not possible for man to be the originator of knowing or the arbiter of what is true knowledge (good) and what are false assertions about knowledge (evil). Man might assert that it is possible, just as he might assert that twice two equals five. But this assertion will spoil that original perfection of orientation toward rest in God that we read about in the first creation account. In other words, "You shall die."

You participate in knowledge, God tells the human, but you do not create it. You are given the garden to live in, but you may not do with it as you will. You did not create it. It is for you and your enjoyment, but it is not yours. Therefore, you have neither the authority nor the ability to determine how it shall be governed. And even to the extent that you can sustain it, you are participating in sustaining something the existence of which is beyond your ability or authority.

But why did God put the tree in the garden to tempt the human? Rather than tell him it is not possible (authentically) to eat from it, why not prevent him from doing so? The answer to these questions goes to the heart of what it means to say that the human is a "moral" creature. And it is perhaps the most important answer for our consideration of moral deliberation and choice.

From the first creation account, we know that God created the human person in his own image and likeness (see Gn 1:26). In the second account, the tree of knowledge of good and evil is a symbol of what that (at least in part) means. In short, unlike any other animal, the human animal is a *moral* creature. By "moral" in this context I do not necessarily mean "good." Rather, I mean that only the human creature is capable of action that we describe as worthy of praise or blame. This is because only the human has the capacity to reflect, choose, and act as an expression of reasoned intention. That is, for an action to be a moral action, it must be voluntary. The actor must have been able to make a deliberate choice to act, rather than acting on instinct or out of conditioning.

But even the human creature commits a *moral* action only to the *relative extent* that the action is committed voluntarily. One cannot be coerced to perform a moral action. Nor can one commit a moral action out of ignorance or fear. To be free, an action must be made voluntarily, as an act of the informed will. Only then can we say that the *action* has moral content. St. Thomas Aquinas thus later calls coercion, ignorance, fear, and passion the "enemies" of voluntariness.[12]

This is why it is necessary for the tree of knowledge of good and evil to be in the midst of the garden and available for the human. The tree is good because it is the symbol of man's freedom, and thus of his moral agency. Without it, man is just like the other creatures, incapable of making a moral choice. The tree represents this essential aspect of human moral agency. God did not put the tree in the garden to tempt the man. Rather, God created the man with the capacity to make moral choices. The tree is the symbol of that capacity. It does not cause the human to fall. Rather, it shows us that he has the unique ability to make authentically good moral choices because he has the freedom to make evil ones. But, as noted above, the measure of good is God himself. Man's freedom is the ability to choose the good; it is not the good itself. As I noted in chapter 1 of this book, freedom is the *necessary* condition for a moral act, but it is not the *sufficient* condition for a morally *good* act. A morally good act is one that is made freely and ordered toward the good.

Eden as a Peaceable Community

The first biblical account of creation is one of peace, order, and harmony. The universe is spoken into existence. Thus language, or communication, is at the very heart of the world as created by God. The Gospel of John emphasizes this rational order of the universe: "In the beginning was the Word, and the Word was with God, and the Word was God. He was in the beginning with God. All things came to be through him, and without him nothing came to be" (Jn 1:1–3a). The Greek word Saint John uses,

Logos, can be translated as "word" or "reason." In either case, it indicates that rational communication is built into the very fabric of creation. Or, to put it another way, creation is built upon a foundation of communication.

Of course, the Gospel of John is telling us that the rational Word at the heart of creation is Christ himself. In addition to telling us that the universe is the product of rational communication, the first creation account tells us that the Holy Trinity is an eternal community of Persons. Thus for the human person to be made in the image of God means (among other things) that the human is created for rational community, oriented away from self toward others in the community in a reciprocal conversation of love. As Joseph Ratzinger puts it, humans are the only beings that "God made capable of thinking and praying. ... To be the image of God implies rationality. It is the dynamic that sets the human being in motion toward the totally Other. Hence it means the capacity for relationship; it is the human capacity for God."[13]

The relational nature of the human person is illustrated by the creation of the community of persons in Genesis 2. After creating the man, "God said: It is not good for the man to be alone. I will make a helper suited to him" (Gn 2:18). This leads to the creation of the woman as the completion of the creation of the human person. The natural state of the human being is as a community of persons. Thus it is "good" that man is not alone. This is wonderfully consonant with the creation account in Genesis 1, where "God created mankind in his image; ... male and female he created them" (Gn 1:27).

This communicative aspect of the image of God is reflected by the community of humans in the Garden of Eden. Prior to the fall, the man and woman exist in harmonious union with one another, and ordered toward God as both their origin and end. They come from God and are ordered toward God, and thus necessarily properly ordered toward one another in mutual self-gift. The two are as one. As "beings of word and of love," explains Ratzinger, they are "oriented to giving themselves to the Other and only truly receiving themselves back in real self-giving."[14] This is what is meant by the last verse of Genesis 2: "The man and his wife were both naked, yet they felt no shame." They existed in a state of natural, mutually self-giving community.

It is important to note that the man and woman in the Garden are aware of their moral agency. They know that they have the choice to eat from the tree of knowledge of good and evil. But, at least to this point, they have used that moral agency in the way it was intended: to choose communion with God and one another, communion in which there is no shame.

The Fall

By introducing the serpent in chapter 3, the Genesis author is more fully illustrating the possibility of moral choice. The "risk" that God took in creating the human with moral agency is that he would use it to choose against the good. But the act of choosing against the good is not just rejecting a particular moral precept. Rather, it is to reject the source and norm of good altogether. We see this in the dialogue between the serpent and the woman in chapter 3:

> Now the serpent was the most cunning of all the beasts of the field that the LORD God had made. And he said to the woman, "Though God said, you shall not eat from any tree of the garden —" And the woman said to the serpent, "From the fruit of the garden's trees we may eat, but from the fruit of the tree in the midst of the garden, God has said, 'You shall not eat from it and you shall not touch it, lest you die.'" And the serpent said to the woman, "You shall not be doomed to die. For God knows that

on the day you eat of it your eyes will be opened and you
will become as gods knowing good and evil." (Genesis
3:1–5)[15]

The man and woman in the Garden of Eden represent us. Indeed, they *are* us. They are proxies for the whole of humanity,
illustrating not just a particular moment in a particular narrative but the entirety of human existence. The dialogue between
the serpent and Eve is the paradigm of the universal occurrence
of our own inner conversations when we are justifying some
thought or moral action that we know to be questionable or
wrong. Put another way, the dialogue between the serpent and
Eve is a representation of our own rationalization for committing sin. But not just that. It is choosing evil and calling it good.
That is the justification.

The serpent, then, can be seen as a symbol of the conscience
of the woman. As she probes the boundaries of moral agency,
she discovers that to be a moral being necessarily entails the possibility of using one's freedom to choose against the good. It is
noteworthy that part of the serpent's reply to the woman is true,
although it is a true utterance used for a deceitful end. "God
knows that on the day you eat of it your eyes will be opened and
you will become as gods knowing good and evil" (Gn 3:4). And
after the man and woman eat, God confirms the truth of the serpent's objection: "The human has become like one of us, knowing good and evil."[16] It is crucially important that we understand
what God means by this affirmation of the serpent's own assertion. As discussed above, authentic knowing is a participation in
the mind of God. It is dependent knowing. We do not originate
truth, nor are we the arbitrators of what is true and false. But in
the story, the humans already know what is good before they eat
from the tree of knowledge of good and evil. Everything is good,
including that very tree. Indeed, the tree is the symbol of the

great good that separates the human from the other creatures: moral agency — the freedom to make authentic moral choices.

Adam and Eve put themselves in the place of God by asserting that they do not participate in God's moral knowledge, but are instead the source of that knowledge. The essence of the Fall is to reject that we are creatures and instead assert that we are creators. And, of course, the most important thing that we can create is our own moral world, molded to serve our own selfish ends. Recall the words of Justice Kennedy from *Planned Parenthood v. Casey*: "At the heart of liberty is the right to define one's own concept of existence, of meaning, of the universe, and of the mystery of human life." Having put themselves in the place of God through the exercise of their moral agency, Adam and Eve are no longer ordered toward the good of rest in God. Rather, their orientation is toward their respective selves. They have destroyed their supernatural relationship with God by presuming to put themselves in God's place. As such, they have necessarily destroyed their natural relationship with one another. If one is pointed in the wrong direction — fundamentally disoriented — every other direction is also necessarily off-course.

But, of course, the humans are only "like" God; they are not God. The creature can never be the Creator. Rather, they — we — are "caricatures" of God, "pseudo-gods."[17] This is illustrated by the shame of their nakedness, which can be understood to have two important meanings.

First, the shame of their nakedness illustrates the foolishness and folly of having put themselves in the place of God. Having rejected God as the source of good and put themselves in God's place, Adam and Eve are *exposed* to the new reality of disordered lives. Their shame is a symbol of their exposure as frauds. It is not just a symbol of guilt for having rejected the good, but rather of having rejected the very reality of good. They used their freedom to choose against the good, which is another way of saying that they saw the possibility of making evil the "good" that orders their lives. Not content to choose the good, in eating from the tree the humans asserted for themselves what the good consists of. They would be *autonomous* — "self-ruling." But, of course, this is a delusion. "Sin is, in its essence, a renunciation of the truth. ... They are living in untruth and in unreality. Their lives are mere appearance."[18] And having realized the sheer folly of their hubris, they cannot but be ashamed of their brazen presumption. Their fraud is exposed. They are naked and ashamed.

A second meaning of the shame of their nakedness is the reciprocal realization that they are no longer ordered toward one another in mutual self-gift, but rather see one another as mutual antagonists. The rationality of authentic human community, built upon truthfulness, is exchanged for the irrationality of human antagonism. No longer living in the harmony of community, in which they were naked and unashamed, the man and woman are at enmity with one another. Their original innocence entailed, among other things, the constructive and positive community of their lives together, cemented by mutual self-trust. As "one flesh," they were not ashamed because they did not see one another as alien. But now, disoriented from the good, they are alienated from one another. They do not stop living in relationship with one another. But now the relationship is one of antagonism and suspicion.

This alienation is not simply between humans, but goes all the way down to the relationship of humans with all of creation. By usurping the place of God, we upset the harmonious balance of creation. It has become, in the words of Thomas Hobbes, a war of all against all. In the fall, all human relationships are compromised in the same way that the relationship between God and humans is compromised. In the Catholic Tradition, this is understood as the foundation of all evil and travail. In the liberal tradition, it is understood as human liberation.

Alienation, Antagonism, and the First City

The antagonism resulting from the Fall is illustrated in the account of Cain and Abel. In one short verse we read: "Cain said to his brother Abel, 'Let us go out in the field.' When they were in the field, Cain attacked his brother Abel and killed him" (Gn 4:8). Although the narrative is spare, we can glean some important implications, flowing from the original sin in Genesis 3.

First, Cain used speech ("Let us go out in the field"), not to build a truthful community, but rather to destroy the natural community that exists between persons. We can be confident that Cain did not indicate to Abel that he wanted to take Abel to the field to kill him. Rather, some pretext probably accompanied the invitation. Like the serpent in chapter 3, Cain used language — whose purpose is to make and sustain human community — for the purpose of deception. This is illustrated in Cain's rhetorical answer to God's inquiry as to Abel's whereabouts: "Am I my brother's keeper?" (Gn 4:9). Of course, this rhetorical question is meant as an assertion: "I am not my brother's keeper." Cain did not merely make a bad choice. Rather, he undermined the very foundation of human community. In asserting that he was not his brother's keeper, Cain was not simply lying; he was denying the very social nature of the human person as created by God.

The result of Cain's sin was banishment from the natural order of human community. He was alienated from the earth that was created to sustain him and from human society. This is less punishment than the "natural" outcome of Cain's deliberate choice to use his moral agency not to order his choices toward the good, but rather to declare by his actions that he is the source and measure of the "good."

Sometime after Cain's banishment, he "became the founder of a city, which he named after his son Enoch" (4:17). Saint Augustine famously compared this founding of the first city in the Bible to the founding of Rome. Both were founded by a fratricide, and both represent the disordered love of self. Cain's city might be seen as a metaphor for the alienation that he had caused by his crime against Abel. Ancient cities were surrounded by walls to protect them from intruders. The walls of the city, therefore, represent the alienation of man from man. They are an indication that man no longer lives in peaceable community, built upon truthful communication. Rather, man now lives in a state of isolated self-interest, each in fear of the other. In other words, it is a war of every man against every man.

The Fall Is the Foundation of American Politics

It is difficult to overstate the explanatory power of the stories of the Fall in Genesis 3 and 4. These accounts of the fundamental alienation of the human person from God and from other humans have such a ring of truth that they seem almost self-evident. But, ironically, this alienation is the foundation of American political life, not as something to be regretted, but rather to be celebrated. Adam and Eve's assertion of moral autonomy, together with Cain's rejection of the natural social nature of the human person, symbolically represent the foundation of liberal political theory.

Of course, Catholics believe that chapters 3 and 4 of Genesis describe the Fall of humankind and its aftermath. But we structure our political lives as though the effects of the Fall are the good and true form of human life. To be sure, we try to cover it with a veneer of religious sensibility. But for many of us, the moral autonomy expressed by Adam and Eve, and the rejection of natural community expressed by Cain, are the way we actually order our own moral and political lives.

In the following chapters, I will propose that a recovery of the moral world of Genesis 1 and 2 is a more hopeful way of thinking about social life, because it expresses the truth about man. As the human person is naturally social, we will proceed with a consideration of the four pillars of Catholic social doctrine: the dignity of the human person, the solidarity of all humankind, the subsidiarity structure of social institutions, and the common good. These fundamental doctrines are the base upon which particular aspects of our common moral lives are structured.

Chapter 3
A Better Foundation: Catholic Social Doctrine

The human person is a social creature in his very essence. He is created in and for social relationships. As we read in Genesis, the human person is created as "male and female," and God says, "It is not good for the man to be alone," indicating that neither is complete without the other. This social nature of the human person is an aspect of what it means to be made in the image and likeness of God (see Gn 1:26–27), who is an eternal community of three Persons in one being. This "dynamic of reciprocity that gives life to the 'we' in the human couple, is an image of God."[1]

Thus, as Vatican II's *Gaudium et Spes* notes, "by his innermost nature man is a social being, and unless he relates himself to others he can neither live nor develop his potential."[2] Society is not something extraneous or incidental to human life, but rather is intrinsic to what it means to be human. We are created in and for community. We know ourselves most fully in relationship to others around us. And we do not know ourselves authentically apart from the presence of our fellow human creatures.

It naturally follows that the full integrity of the human person is achieved and recognized only to the extent that his social nature is affirmed and fostered. Thus while we recognize and protect individual moral agency as the necessary condition for moral action, we also affirm that our moral lives are necessarily entwined with the moral lives of our fellows. As the *Compendium of the Social Doctrine of the Church* explains the point: "Sin is composed of a twofold wound, which the sinner opens in his own side and in the relationship with his neighbor. That is why we can speak of personal sin and social sin."[3] Quoting Pope St. John Paul II, the *Compendium* continues, "By virtue of human solidarity ... each individual's sin in some way affects others."[4] This implies that the Church's moral thinking is always concerned with the human person in community with others. All moral doctrine is social doctrine.

Our application of Catholic moral teaching to social and political issues will be framed within the context of Catholic social doctrine. Most scholars recognize that Catholic social doctrine began as a distinct body of theological reflection as recently as 1891, with the promulgation of Pope Leo XIII's landmark encyclical, *Rerum Novarum*.[5] Although the Church's deliberative application of its doctrine to concrete questions of labor and employment, economic structures, environmental issues, political life, and war and peace, among other issues, is a recent development, the fundamental anthropology that informs this body of doctrine is at the very heart of Christian moral thought from its beginning. The truths are as ancient as all Christian doctrine, whose foundation is the creation accounts of Genesis.

Catholic social doctrine is built upon a foundation of four central pillars:

1. The inherent dignity of the human person
2. The solidarity of all humankind
3. The subsidiary nature of social structures
4. The common good

Understood together, these doctrines present a coherent body of teaching that transcends the individualism of American political liberalism, in both its left and right variations. Catholic social doctrine is not a "middle way" between the extremes of American political rhetoric and policy, because it is not on the same continuum. Catholic social doctrine is neither "liberal" nor "conservative," because it does not correspond to the political noun that these partisan adjectives modify. Rather, the Church's social teaching offers a different moral language. It is a language consistent with the nature of the human person, while recognizing that that nature is fallen. This teaching recognizes and protects the integrity of the human person as a moral agent. But it avoids the false story of autonomous individualism that informs the broad spectrum of American politics.

The Inherent Dignity of the Human Person

Human dignity is not the measure of some list of external faculties, attributes, or abilities. Dignity is not earned by the accumulation or expression of talents. It is not surrendered, even by the most egregious acts. Nor is it lost by the deterioration of physical, psychological, or cognitive abilities or faculties. The severely impaired hospice patient has no less dignity than the Nobel Prize winner in the prime of his intellectual power. Simply put, human dignity is not conditioned on anything that we can do, fail to do, or lose the ability to do. It is intrinsic to the human person by virtue of being made in the image and likeness of God and ordered toward rest in his love. The relative capacity or ability to exercise the attributes that we associate with the image of God cannot change that central truth about human dignity.

Still, we often behave in ways that are inconsistent with our dignity. While it cannot be taken from us, we can act in ways that make it appear as though we are not ordered toward love of God. To paraphrase Saint Paul in his Letter to the Romans, all have sinned and fallen short of their human dignity (see 3:23). But to fall short is not to cancel out. Dignity is both a gift and a summons. It is the gift of unique communion with God, and it is the challenge to form our lives consistently with that communion. Sin is not a renunciation or abandonment of dignity, but rather an offense against it. When we sin, we bear false witness to our inherent dignity. Dignity can be compromised; it cannot be lost.

This foundational teaching of Catholic social doctrine has broad public policy implications. From abortion to euthanasia, from immigration to capital punishment, from education to health care, from marriage to same-sex attraction and gender confusion, recourse to the inherent, inalienable dignity of the human person is a necessary guiding principle for moral choices and public policy positions. It informs our deliberation, giving us a strong presumption for a consideration of most legal, regulatory, or political questions. It can serve both as a starting point and limiting principle to how we think about and advocate for public policy positions. And, of course, an unwavering commitment to the dignity of every person should strongly inform our own moral lives.

This fundamental commitment to dignity does not fit either of the two major political parties in the United States.

Aspects of Human Dignity

Dignity is not simply an abstract, academic category to be debated among theologians. Like every aspect of moral theology, dignity is not about theory, but rather about human action and development. The doctrine of human dignity has concrete implications for moral choices and political deliberation. Specifically, dignity implies (at least) two broad considerations: 1) transcendence and moral agency and 2) fundamental equality.

1. The search for transcendence

Walker Percy's novel *The Moviegoer* is the story of a Korean War veteran and New Orleans stockbroker, Binx Bolling, and his "search." Binx describes the first time the search occurred to him, when he had been wounded in battle and was pressed against the ground, unable to move. "Six inches from my nose a dung beetle was scratching around under the leaves," Binx explains. "As I watched, there awoke in me an immense curiosity. I was onto something. I vowed that if I ever got out of this fix, I would pursue the search." But like many such vows, he concedes, "Naturally, as soon as I recovered and got home, I forgot all about it."[6] But ten years later, the "possibility of a search" occurs to him while he is dressing for the day. As he prepares to put the usual items in his pockets (wallet, notebook, keys), Binx recounts, "they looked both unfamiliar and at the same time full of clues. I stood in the center of the room and gazed at the little pile. … What was unfamiliar about them was that I could see them. They might have belonged to someone else. A man can look at this little pile on his bureau for thirty years and never once see it. It is as invisible as his own hand. Once I saw it, however, the search became possible."[7]

The idea of the search occurs to him again that morning as he rides a bus to visit his aunt. "The truth is I dislike cars," Binx says. "Whenever I drive a car, I have a feeling I have become invisible. People on the street cannot see you; they only watch your rear fender until it is out of their way."[8]

These impressions might be called "alienation." In the "everydayness" of his life, Binx has become psychologically separated from the things and people that tell him who he is. He does not recognize his things because he does not recognize himself. Nor, he thinks, is he recognized by others as he goes about his day. Binx explains the point: "The search is what anyone would undertake if he were not sunk in the everydayness of his own life. ... To become aware of the possibility of the search is to be onto something. Not to be onto something is to be in despair."[9]

Percy's contention, as set forth in the novel, is that the modern person has lost his sense of transcendence. He has lost his sense of self as uniquely known through the various signposts that give shape and meaning to his life. He does not know himself. But, in his delightfully whimsical character Binx Bolling, Percy shows us that we have not lost the *capacity* for transcendence, elusive as it might seem.

In his nonfiction book *Lost in the Cosmos*, Percy more directly accounts both for our capacity for transcendence and our lost sense of what that entails about who we are. "How do you explain these odd little phenomena with which everyone is familiar?" he asks.

> You have seen yourself a thousand times in the mirror, face to face. No sight is more familiar. Yet why is it that the first time you see yourself in a clothier's triple mirror — from the side, so to speak — it comes as a shock? ...
>
> Why is it that when you are shown a group photograph in which you are present, you always (and probably covertly) seek yourself out? To see what you look like? Don't you know what you look like?[10]

Through these and other questions, Percy accounts both for the transcendent dignity of the human person and our inability to understand what it means. We *can* know ourselves, but we do not. We are alienated from ourselves because we are alienated from God. As Percy explains, the "Christian self" is "created by God, estranged from God ... and now reconciled with him." As such, this self "is conscious of itself as a creature of God embarked upon a pilgrimage in this life and destined for happiness and reunion with God in a later life."[11] But with "the fading of Christianity as a guarantor of the identity of the self, the self becomes distorted ... is both cut loose and imprisoned by its own freedom."[12]

The human person has the unique ability to make abstractions about himself — to think about selfhood. This is in contrast to all other animals, which have neither the capacity to wonder nor to "think" about themselves as selves. The gift of transcendence that attends our dignity is a great gift, but it carries a great responsibility. As Percy was aware, it may fill us with joy or dread, depending on a proper or improper understanding of its implication. The German philosopher Friedrich Nietzsche illustrates this point in a famous passage from his essay, "On the Use and Abuse of History for Life":

> Consider the herds that are feeding yonder: they know not the meaning of yesterday or today; they graze and ruminate, move or rest, from morning to night from day to day ... at the mercy of the moment, feeling neither melancholy nor satiety. Man cannot see them without regret, for even in the pride of his humanity he looks enviously on the beast's happiness. [Man] wishes simply to live without satiety or pain, like the beast; yet it is all in vain, for he will not change places with it. He may ask the beast, "Why do you look at me and not speak to me of your happiness?" The beast wants to answer, "Because I always forget what I wished to say"; but he forgets this

answer too, and is silent. *And the man is left to wonder.*[13]

For Nietzsche, the capacity of man to wonder — to transcend himself — should fill us with dread and despair, because we have the capacity to wonder, but nothing to wonder about. Man "also wonders about himself, that he cannot learn to forget, but hangs on to the past: however far he can run, that chain runs with him," he continues. "It is matter for wonder: the moment, that is here and gone, that was nothing before and nothing after, returns like a specter to trouble the quiet of a later moment."[14] Nietzsche was half right. Man's capacity for transcendence must be properly ordered and practiced, but it is not a specter; it is a gift. Like any other human ability, it can be neglected and, thus, compromised from its fullness.

Yet our sense of transcendence is not limited to contemplation of personhood — the ability to abstract from the self to think about what *self* even means. Rather, the full capacity for transcendence also entails the ability to contemplate the reality beyond what we can see and feel with our physical senses or imagine in our own persons. It necessarily entails the ability to know others, and to form emotional, psychological, and spiritual relationships with others. Most importantly, to be made in the image and likeness of God is to be created with the capacity to *know* God. Our sense of wonder has a proper object in God himself, toward whom it is ordered. Simply put, the human person has the capacity to worship, to seek and find good that transcends all created things.

As we will see in chapters 4 and 5, this has important implications for a number of public policy issues. For now, it will be sufficient to note three general conclusions to be drawn from the transcendent dignity of the human person. The first is that the capacity to worship must not merely be protected, but encouraged and incentivized. Worship of God is a public good, contributing to the flourishing of the human person. As such, legal, political, and public policy decisions should have a presumption in favor of facilitating worship and the leisure that worship requires. This has special implications for policy related to work and economic life.

Second, the transcendence that accompanies human dignity implies respect for and protection of the subjectivity of the human person. The human person is not a mere object to be acted upon, but rather a dynamic *subject*, with the capacity to reflect, judge, and choose. The development of subjective moral agency should be inherent in every consideration of moral action and public policy. As such, the human person may never be used merely as an object — as the means to some end. We are not to be reduced to our utilitarian usefulness. Thus we are not to be used for the good of another; nor are we to be discarded or disregarded if we are determined to have no public utility. The transcendence necessarily implied by human dignity is the moral mandate to value the human person from conception to natural death.

Third, the inherent subjectivity of the person necessarily implies that the person is a moral agent, whose ability to make moral choices must be protected and fostered. When our ability to exercise moral agency is inhibited, the moral quality of our choices is compromised. This does not imply that the liberty to make a moral choice is the sum and substance of morality. But liberty is the necessary condition for a moral action. And it is rooted in the subjectivity of the human person, which itself is a characteristic of our dignity. This has important policy implications for a number of public institutions and actions, including business, education, and health care, to name a few.

2. *Equality of dignity*
Dignity is not relative to the abilities or inabilities of particular persons. Dignity is not indexed to moral behavior, social status, intellectual competency, physical dexterity, or emotional stability. Every human person exists somewhere on a continuum of

these and other attributes. But one's dignity does not rise or fall according to his place on the range of particular relative human characteristics. This has important policy implications that do not fit into either major political party or the moral sentiments that either produce.

While many pay lip service to the dignity of the human person, policy discussions and decisions often abandon the principle for some other purported good. As Pope St. John Paul II put it, on the one hand, we have "a growing moral sensitivity, more alert to acknowledging the value and dignity of every individual as a human being, without any distinction of race, nationality, religion, political opinion or social class." But, he observes, these noble sentiments are often "contradicted by a tragic repudiation of them in practice."[15] We Catholics must remain diligent lest we contradict our commitment to the dignity of the person by repudiating it in our moral choices, even (if not especially) when we advocate for political and policy outcomes.

For example, as a person ages, his physical abilities will always decline, and some of his cognitive abilities may as well. Eventually, both these functions may regress to the point at which he is barely able to care for himself, if at all. If we measure dignity by these declining abilities, we might say that this person has "less dignity" than he did when he was cognitively sharp and physiologically vigorous. But, of course, he is same person, made in the same image and likeness of God. Nothing has changed about his essential being. While his ability to participate fully in the image of God varies, the God who made him with that dignity does not. Nor does the dignity in which he was made.

Or take a person born into dire poverty in a developing country with an authoritative government. By the circumstances of her birth (which she no more chose than I chose mine), she will be denied educational opportunities, nutrition, hydration, medical care, and perhaps even liberty to speak, read, and travel.

All these deficiencies will impede her ability to develop the personal attributes that we might cavalierly think must be present for her to have the same dignity as a person born to economic privilege in a prosperous nation. Of course, this would be a dire mistake. The relative disadvantages of her birth and developmental environment are separate from her dignity as a being made in the image and likeness of God. Her dignity is equal to the dignity of the person in the wealthy nation who enjoys the blessings of economic prosperity and political liberty.

Of course, few readers of this book would expressly articulate an opinion that a person has less dignity because of the circumstance of her birth. But do we proactively *affirm* that dignity when we think about issues related to immigration, for example, or international aid? Or are we more likely to advocate for policy positions that seem to imply that she is somehow less dignified because of the accident of her birth? And is that implicit impulse a product of our Catholic Faith or our commitment to a particular political party?

A less sympathetic example might be someone who has committed a particularly gruesome crime. To be certain, his actions are not consistent with his dignity. He has compromised his participation in the image and likeness of God, and we are understandably horrified and repulsed by his behavior. In the interest of both public safety and the hope of his rehabilitation, we are justified in depriving him of the property and liberty to which he might otherwise be entitled. But we cannot deny his fundamental and inalienable dignity. Has he been a false witness to his dignity? Certainly. But so have I. So have you. Even when we are forced to incarcerate or otherwise penalize a person for disturbing the public peace or, by his actions, denying the dignity of another, our actions must begin with that fundamental dignity, which cannot be lost, even though its effects can be compromised.

Each of these cases describes a very different subjective experience, with very different causes. Yet none of these experiences has any bearing on the fundamental nature of the persons described. To be sure, their abilities or choices are not as relatively consonant with their dignity or the dignity of others. But dignity is the very measure by which we make that judgment. Our moral response, therefore, should be motivated not by their subjective perfection, but by their objective being.

As I discuss below, the range of legitimate legal, political, and policy debates may be wide. People of good will may disagree. But if the disagreement is not rooted in the fundamental equal dignity of all human persons, it is misguided from the start. As Catholics, our contribution to the debate must begin with the objective dignity of the human person and proceed from there. Questions of public safety, scarcity of medical resources, national security, and immigration policy, to name a few, are all legitimate points of discussion. But the discussion must be conducted within the context of the inherent dignity of the human person. We might compromise on policy decisions; we cannot compromise on human dignity.

The Solidarity of All Humankind

As noted earlier in this book, our consideration of Catholic moral doctrine always returns to the first few chapters of Genesis. The creation accounts are a rich trove of moral teaching, including the teaching on solidarity. Both creation accounts suggest the doctrine of solidarity of all humankind. In the first, Genesis 1:27 simply declares, "God created man in his image; in the image of God he created him; male and female he created them." The human person shares in the essential social nature of the Triune God: the eternal fellowship of love among Father, Son, and Holy Spirit. As an "image" of God, the human person shares certain essential attributes with God, including this social nature. An initial consideration of the importance of this gives us an indication of the importance of the doctrine of solidarity.

It is not possible for any of the Persons of the Holy Trinity to be in tension or disagreement with any other, or to turn against or abandon one another. Such a notion is not even imaginable. The solidarity of the Holy Trinity, three divine Persons in one divine being, is eternally inseparable. This is illustrated even in the Garden of Gethsemane, when Jesus says, "Father, if you are willing, take this cup away from me" (Lk 22:42a). As fully man, Jesus experiences many of the same temptations and impulses toward weakness that we all experience. He is not one "who is unable to sympathize with our weaknesses, but one who has similarly been tested in every way, yet without sin" (Heb 4:15). But in the same breath, Jesus says, "Still, not my will but yours be done" (Lk 22:42b). This is because the will of the Holy Trinity is no more divisible than God himself. Solidarity is an intrinsic quality of the Triune God. Made in his image, the human person participates in that solidarity. We look to it as a model for structuring our own lives together.

The second creation account in Genesis 2 similarly suggests the doctrine of solidarity. Using a different literary style, the author of the second chapter gets us to the same conclusion as the first. "It is not good for the man to be alone," God says. "I will make a helper suited tor him" (v. 18). Ultimately, no partner is suitable for the man other than the one taken from his very being. "This one ... is bone of my bones and flesh of my flesh" (v. 23).

The man says, "This one shall be called 'woman' [Hebrew *ishah*] for out of man [Hebrew *ish*] this one has been taken" (v. 23) — a Hebrew pun. This tells us that the one is not complete without the other, and that the other is only known in reference to the one. I use the terms *one* and *other* in this context to emphasize that the humans are both dependent upon and known in relation to one another, without regard to the different (though complementary) sexes. For the purposes of this consideration, dependency and identity are the essential points. This description of the essential social nature of the human person is the basis for the Church's understanding of solidarity.

Denial of Solidarity and Human Alienation

Of course, this all comes undone in Genesis 3. But the Fall does not obliterate the social nature of the human person. Rather, the Fall is the rupture of the solidarity for which we are naturally created. The alienation of the man and woman is not their natural state, but rather their fallen state. The task of the moral life in Christ, then, is to work toward the restoration of the solidarity of all human beings. This has profound importance for a host of political, legal, and social issues, including employee/employer relationships, immigration policy, penal reform, the nature of the family, and health care policy, among other public issues.

The *Catechism of the Catholic Church* refers to solidarity as a "virtue" (see 1942, 1948). As such, like any other virtue, solidarity develops through the practices and habits of moral agents. It is both essential to the human being and the virtue by which our fallen social nature is to be restored. The solidarity of all human persons is the mandate to structure our moral lives consistently with that nature. As Pope St. John Paul II put it in his encyclical *Sollicitudo Rei Socialis*, solidarity is "not a feeling of vague compassion or shallow distress. ... On the contrary, it is a firm and persevering determination to commit oneself to the common good; that is to say the good of all ... because we are all really responsible for all."[16] This is echoed by Pope Francis, who explains in *Fratelli Tutti*, "Solidarity means much more than engaging in sporadic acts of generosity. It means thinking and acting in terms of community. It means that the lives of all are prior to the appropriation of goods by a few."[17] Considered this way, solidarity is rooted in the virtue of justice — rendering to another his due. As common members of the one human race, we are responsible for one another. As a virtue, solidarity is "a commitment to the good of one's neighbor with the readiness … to 'lose oneself' for the sake of the other."[18]

Again, this causes us to return to the Book of Genesis, this time to chapter 4. When Cain slew Abel, God asked Cain, "Where is your brother?" Cain's response was less an answer than an assertion: "I do not know. Am I my brother's keeper?" (Gn 4:9). Even apart from the murder of his brother, Cain's action symbolizes the alienation of man from man when he denies the truth of his social nature. Rather than affirm solidarity with his brother, Cain separates himself from Abel. The "natural" result of this rejection of solidarity is Cain's own banishment from the community of others. As a "constant wanderer on the earth" (v. 12), Cain is alienated from all other people. And since solidarity means that we only know ourselves in relationship to others, Cain is alienated from himself. This alienation is symbolized when Cain builds the first city, which, like all ancient cities, would have had thick, tall walls, separating those within from those without. When solidarity is denied or compromised, alienation follows.

Christ as the Man for Others

As with all other effects of the Fall, the remedy for the alienation of man from man is found in the life, death, and resurrection of Christ. In his Person, Jesus is the literal embodiment of the restoration of solidarity between God and man and between man and his fellow man. "By his Incarnation the Son of God has united himself in some fashion with every man," explains *Gaudium et Spes*. "He worked with human hands, He thought with a human mind, acted by human choice and loved with a human heart. Born of the Virgin Mary, He has truly been made one of us, like us in all things except sin."[19] Jesus, who knew no sin, took on all effects of sin in his Person. This includes the alienation that comes from of our denial of solidarity.

Jesus is the "man for others," showing us that the nature and purpose of the human person is to live for others, giving of oneself without expectation of return. This notion of "self-gift" is the ultimate expression of restored solidarity. By giving himself for us, Christ demonstrates the perfection of solidarity, which we are called to emulate in our relationships with others. "What does this solidarity consist of?" asks Pope St. John Paul II. "This union with us in humanity on the part of Jesus Christ, *true man*, is the fundamental expression of his solidarity with every man," he answers.

> *Love is reconfirmed here in a very particular way*: The one who loves wants to *share everything with the beloved*. Precisely for this reason the Son of God becomes man. ... This "love-solidarity" stands out in the whole life and earthly mission of the Son of Man *in relation, above all, to those who suffer* under the weight of any type of physical or moral misery.[20]

In subsequent chapters, we will explore some concrete implications of the virtue of solidarity. This consideration will challenge us to think beyond the categories of modern politics because solidarity is a concept that does not fit anywhere within the spectrum of American political or legal life. Yes, we can find instances of political, legal, or social institutions that are consistent with a rigorous doctrine of solidarity. But these incidental forms are usually not informed by what we Catholics understand by the doctrine set forth in this chapter. On the contrary, the moral and political theory at the heart of American politics *denies* the solidarity of all humankind in favor of isolated individualism.

Subsidiarity: Solidarity's Mirror Virtue

Of the four pillars of Catholic social doctrine, two are so closely related that they might be thought of as twin or mirror principles. The virtue of solidarity discussed above must always be considered together with the principle of subsidiarity. For purposes of public policy decisions, especially, these two doctrines contribute to a full consideration of the propriety of social decision-making. In the simplest terms, subsidiarity is the principle that social issues should be addressed by the smallest, closest, and least complex structure as practicable. Its most famous formulation is from Pope Pius XI's 1931 social encyclical, *Quadragesimo Anno*:

> Just as it is gravely wrong to take from individuals what they can accomplish by their own initiative and industry and give it to the community, so also it is an injustice and at the same time a grave evil and disturbance of right order to assign to a greater and higher association what lesser and subordinate organizations can do. For every social activity ought of its very nature to furnish help to the members of the body social, and never destroy and absorb them.[21]

Remote or complex social structures exist for the purpose of *helping* (*"subsidium"*) proximate and less complex structures, not for the purpose of taking over their functions. Again, in the words of *Quadragesimo Anno*:

> The supreme authority of the State ought, therefore, to let subordinate groups handle matters and concerns of lesser importance, which would otherwise dissipate its efforts greatly. Thereby the State will more freely, powerfully, and effectively do all those things that belong to

it alone because it alone can do them: directing, watching, urging, restraining, as occasion requires and necessity demands.[22]

This is a useful beginning definition of *subsidiarity*. To fully appreciate its purpose and function in Catholic moral theology, however, we must consider what goods the doctrine of subsidiarity serves. A common misconception is that subsidiarity is merely another name for limited government or even libertarian politics. It is sometimes described in terms that seem to make it nothing more than a tool for maximizing personal autonomy, expressed in possessive individual rights. Properly applied, subsidiarity does indeed have the effect of curbing excesses of some kinds of social institutions and decentralizing policy-making. But this is incidental to the purpose of the doctrine. The end of subsidiarity is not to limit government for the sake of maximizing individual rights. Rather, its purpose is to expand human moral agency for the moral development of the person. The distinction is subtle but very important.

When I criticize the use of "rights language," I am often asked what I would replace this language with for the protection of individual freedom. Is not liberty an authentic value? And are not "rights" the moral category by which individual liberty is protected in the modern, liberal state? "We hold these truths to be self-evident, that all men ... are endowed by their Creator with certain unalienable Rights." Informed by this assertion in every aspect of private and public life, we Americans believe that God has created us with individual claims to do as we will in the pursuit of "Life, Liberty and the pursuit of Happiness."

Of course, when the average person uses the language of "rights," he is not thinking of the theory of Thomas Hobbes and other originators of this radical new moral theory. Instead, one may think of rights as the moral framework by which individuals are protected from coercion. Rights in this understanding are the insulation from being compelled to act against one's conscience. Or rights might be thought of as a set of political or legal goods, such as the right to drive a car, buy a house, marry the person of one's choice, or live where one wishes. All these are things that are indeed social goods. But we do not need the liberal theory of individual rights to secure them.

On the contrary, the moral theory in which a language of individual rights is rooted is corrosive of the privileges, immunities, and protections that rights are supposed to protect. This is because individual rights language is rooted in the false moral anthropology of radical individualism that is not compatible with the Catholic virtue of solidarity. Divorced from a moral anthropology of solidarity, rights become the chief weapon in the "war of all against all" in Thomas Hobbes's "state of nature." Rather than signifying the natural community for which we are created, rights language signifies all the ramifications of the alienation that has resulted from the Fall. The cruel irony of a moral language reflective of radical individualism is that it leads to toxic tribalism, the claims of which can only be adjudicated by ever-encroaching state power.[23]

One might object at this point that many magisterial Church documents are replete with the language of human rights. A sampling across the spectrum of the official documents of Catholic social teaching will support this objection. As early as 1891, in *Rerum Novarum*, the rights of workers and families are discussed at some length. And this language persists through the great teaching documents of Vatican II, and all the popes since. Indeed, it seems as though "rights language" is the core moral category of modern Catholic moral thought. But the way rights language is used in virtually all these documents is quite different from the way it is used in modern liberal political theory. In Catholic teaching, "rights" are always rooted in the fundamental dignity of the human person, and are thought of as protections against threats to that dignity. In other words, rights in Church teaching are not claims to every thing and against every one. Rather, the word *rights* signifies the inherent dignity of the person and, thus, the impropriety of actions by individuals or governments that violate that dignity.

Put another way, rights in Church documents are almost always carefully rooted in the primary reciprocal duties that we owe to one another, rather than the claims that we have against one another. This is illustrated, for example, in *Dignitatis Humanae*, Vatican II's Declaration on Religious Liberty. The "right" to religious freedom is nothing other than a corollary of the duty of the human person to practice the virtue of religion.

With its commitment to the solidarity of the human person, Catholic moral theology might mistakenly be thought to ignore the importance of the individual. Or worse, if not properly understood, the doctrine of solidarity might seem to subsume individual identity (and thus dignity) into the collective, such that the good of the individual person is completely lost. If this were the case, individual liberty might indeed be lost in a false notion of social collectivism. The answer to this objection is the doctrine of subsidiarity, which, when coupled with solidarity, produces a robust moral foundation for the proper balancing of social interests consistent with the integrity and dignity of the individual person.

Subsidiarity protects the moral agency of the human person. "Agency" is a better way of accounting for and protecting the implications of human dignity than the language of rights, even when the latter is rooted in something like a proper understanding of human dignity. *Agency* is the word we use to account for an individual person's exercise of a moral action. As noted in chapter 1, for an action to be properly moral, it must be chosen free from coercion. The extent that human action is free from constraint is precisely the extent to which moral agency is pro-tected. Importantly, however, the principle of agency is not just about freedom from constraint. A theory of agency also must respect the broad scope of the moral life, giving as much berth as possible to authentic moral choices and, thus, authentic moral teaching. Agency is not only about acting free from coercion, but also about expanding and preserving the space that individuals must have to make moral decisions and commit moral acts.

In Catholic moral theology, morality is not reduced merely to the object chosen. The object is important, of course, but a full consideration of the morality of an action also takes into account both the intention and the circumstance of the moral actor. This is because the moral life is not simply about making the right choice or choosing the right moral object. Rather, Catholic moral theology is concerned with becoming the right kind of person. One develops the moral skills that we call *virtues* through voluntary, deliberative choices of the right object, *in the right manner*. As such, moral action doesn't simply achieve some object, but rather develops the moral character of a person through the practices that accompany achieving the proper object. That is, Catholic moral theology is concerned with the development of the person as a moral agent, fully engaged in the reflective consideration at the heart of moral decision-making. When these aspects of moral development are assumed by structures and institutions, they detract from this development, and thus violate the principle of subsidiarity and frustrate its purpose.

For example, a person may contribute money or property to some person or organization in sincere need. The contribution from one's wealth is the moral object. But this does not tell us anything about why one made the property transfer, or what one's disposition was when he made it. Let's say that the transfer is a forced distribution through the threat of some sanction if it is not made, such as taxation. Or perhaps it is made not for the good of the recipient but for some advantage of the giver. He made the gift to avoid some other cost or even to achieve some benefit, such as recognition or fame. In either case, the donation itself is still a good object. The recipient was in need, and the transfer of wealth met that need. But we cannot say that the moral action of making the transfer was the same kind of action as if the distribution were motivated solely by a charitable impulse for the good of the recipient. That is because (in addition to the object) both the intention of the giver and the circumstance of the gift are necessary considerations for the judgment of a moral action. All of which is to say that the moral agency of the giver is always a central consideration, both in his choice to make the gift and the development of his own moral character in making it.

Agency implies at least two things. First, individuals must be free to commit moral acts. Second, the range of the possibility of committing moral actions must be as broad as practicably possible. Subsidiarity preserves these two aspects of agency. As such, subsidiarity serves the development of robust, thriving social and community institutions, which are created by and in turn serve to support the full development of the human person. It is not the purpose of subsidiarity to limit government. Rather, its purpose is to protect the moral development of the human person. This development necessarily requires the moral space for the human person to exercise his own moral judgment and action. In the chapters that follow, I will discuss some concrete applications of this principle, especially as it applies to the distinction between political life and other forms of social or civic life.

Subsidiarity suggests the default position that small and local is better than large and remote. Sometimes, however, social challenges or issues can only be addressed by remote and complex agencies or organizations. Large-scale pandemics or other

national emergencies, for example, might require more centralized solutions than otherwise might be indicated. Indeed, even
Pope Pius XI's famous explanation of the principle of subsidiarity suggests that some social problems can only be addressed
by large-scale institutions. "As history abundantly proves," wrote
the pope, "it is true that on account of changed conditions many
things which were done by small associations in former times
cannot be done now save by large associations."[24]

The test of subsidiarity is not whether the solution is remote
or proximate, or whether it is simple or complex. Rather, it is
whether the institution properly serves the development of the
moral agency of the human person in vigorous and numerous
civic spaces. Indeed, where centralized structures better serve
human agency (as sometimes is the case), subsidiarity is still
observed. The question of when larger institutions better serve
human flourishing can sometimes be a difficult one, requiring
sound prudential judgment, often formed in the crucible of
democratic debate. But the principle to be served is the moral
development of the human person. Human dignity, not smaller
government, is the purpose of subsidiarity.

Generally speaking, however, the principle of subsidiarity
suggests a strong presumption in favor of decentralized political
and legal authority for the purpose of fostering strong, vibrant
civic and social institutions. Usually, the role of larger institutions, including state and federal agencies, will be to institute
laws and regulations that encourage, support, and facilitate the
development of nonpolitical civic institutions. Families, churches, social clubs and organizations, community centers, fraternal
societies, and other voluntary associations are at the heart of
moral development. Those institutions serve the robust development of conscientious moral agents, consistent with the principle of common good, the fourth principle of Catholic social
doctrine.

The Common Good

When properly considered and balanced with one another, solidarity and subsidiarity contribute to the social principle of common good. As Vatican II's *Gaudium et Spes* puts it, the "political community exists … for the sake of the common good, in which it finds its full justification and significance, and the source of its inherent legitimacy."[25] This teaching is a useful reminder that the Catholic understanding of the role of political life is very different from liberalism. Politics is not simply concerned with the protection of purported individual rights, or redress when such rights are violated. Modern liberalism (from the right to the left) sees itself as nothing other than a set of procedural rules, not imposing any particular vision of the good. No such politics exists, despite assertions of the liberal myth. All politics is substantive, regardless of its provenance or claims.

But while *Gaudium et Spes* tells us that politics has a proper interest in achieving the common good, *defining* the common good is not a simple task. As with solidarity and subsidiarity, it is useful to begin a definition of the common good by describing what it is not. Just as solidarity is not collectivism and subsidiarity is not individualism, the common good is neither the absorption of the individual into the collective nor simply the measure of accumulations of individual goods, especially economic or material goods.

Certainly, for the common good to be achieved, certain levels of material wealth and economic vitality are required. Some quantifiable goods such as access to housing, health care, education, nutrition, and leisure to worship are necessary, constitutive elements of the common good. But the common good is not achieved merely by the attainment of a minimum level of material prosperity. It cannot be reduced to a calculation or spreadsheet.

Nor is the common good simply the measure of the distribution (or redistribution) of wealth. Significant disparities of wealth may be an indicator that the common good has not been achieved in a particular political economy. And certain tools for regulating wealth accumulation or effecting redistribution may be necessary, constitutive elements of the common good. But absent a host of other goods — some quantifiable and some not — merely redistributing wealth to achieve something like relative equality will not achieve the common good. *Common good* is not simply another name for some goal of the welfare state or redistributive regulatory structures.

An additional problem with defining and discussing the common good in the modern liberal context is that liberal politics denies the very reality of "common" good. Instead, liberalism suggests that politics is merely a procedural structure under which individuals may pursue any number of competing visions of the good, so long as one's version of the good does not molest another in his pursuit. Again, this is a pernicious and persistent myth. There is no such thing as merely procedural politics. Liberalism is built upon the *substantive* vision of man as radically solitary in his essence, in direct contradiction to the Catholic understanding of the social nature of the person and the solidarity of all humankind. In the same way, for many advocates of liberalism, the "common good" is nothing other than the imposition of a collectivist vision of politics, incompatible with the robust liberal vision. To speak a Catholic language of common good is by and large to speak a language that American politics rejects.

So, defining the common good is difficult even within the context of Catholic moral theology. And it is a moral and political concept that is largely rejected by modern politics from across the American spectrum. Perhaps the best we can do, then, is to describe aspects of our lives together that are consistent with dignity, solidarity, and subsidiarity, and conclude that, to the extent that we can achieve policies consistent with those values, we have approximated the common good. Put another way, perhaps the best way to define the common good is as a state of affairs in which dignity, solidarity, and subsidiarity are acknowledged and approximately achieved. If, theoretically, we live in a society in which true visions of dignity, solidarity, and subsidiarity are observed and achieved, it seems almost necessarily to follow that the common good would obtain. And if this sounds hopelessly vague and abstract, I am hopeful that the following chapters will offer some clear and concrete descriptions through a consideration of the social institutions of family, church, work, economics, and politics.

Before moving on to the concrete consideration noted above, we will conclude with a refinement of our description of the common good that at least accounts for those human goods that cannot be measured or quantified. Elusive as the common good might be to define, we can at least account for features of it to guide our way. Quoting *Gaudium et Spes* (26), the *Catechism* describes the common good as "the sum total of social conditions which allow people, either as groups or as individuals, to reach their fulfillment more fully and more easily" (1906). This fulfillment, of course, is not met merely by the attainment of material goods. Rather, material goods are necessary for the creation of those conditions by which nonmaterial goods may be obtained. The material goods do not themselves create the conditions. To provide the means is not to achieve the task.

Because the good is "common," it cannot be diminished by being shared. The social conditions by which the human person is able to pursue fulfillment must be the same for all, or else it is not "common," but rather merely diverse. Nor is it divisible, as though some people may have a greater quantity of "common" good than others. To be sure, the common good may be approximated even in the presence of some degree of inequality. But the common good itself — and the minimum social conditions that make it possible — must be available to all. This is the mandate for all persons to work for the good of others as though it were our own good. If the common good is truly common — and if it is not diminished by being shared — then we all have a moral mandate to pursue it for others as though as for ourselves. When it is (approximately) achieved for one, it is no less achieved for all.

Moreover, if the common good is the achievement of the conditions for true human fulfillment, some laws, policies, and public institutions can never be compatible with the common good. Euthanasia, abortion, contraception, torture, pornography, prostitution, surrogate parenting, capital punishment, and restrictions on freedom of religion, assembly, and travel are all detrimental to authentic human fulfillment and flourishing. While some of these things may sometimes be subject to democratic compromise, the requirements of the common good give us Catholics a mandate to work toward changing hearts, minds, laws, and regulations such that they are more consistent with genuine human development. One cannot simultaneously be committed to the common good and affirm any of these social maladies.

Chapter 4
The Family: The First Subsidiarity Society

The 2021 Grammy award for best country song went to "Crowded Table," from the debut album of The Highwomen.[1] On the one hand, the song is a celebration of the family as a resilient community of love and fellowship. It acknowledges that the various members of the family must eventually go their way in the world, to exercise their own moral agency. At the end of the proverbial day, however, may the ties that bind them bring them back to the family table, and to gather around the fire. Yet for this to happen, work must be done, as the song makes clear: We have to give love, the song explains, if that's what we want to find in our family. Yes, the family is a natural community (as I will explain below), but it requires proactive cultivation by its various members to fulfill its purpose as a community of reciprocal love.

On the other hand, however, "Crowded Table" is a concession to the frailty both of the family and its various members. As no person is without sin, so no family is perfect. The test, the song suggests, is not whether the family is faultless, but rather whether it is welcoming of those who have fallen, recognizing that we are all on the same continuum of brokenness and alienation. The family is a source of consolation and forgiveness, rooted in the transparency and self-realization that we are all in need of reconciliation at some point. No matter how alienated some members may feel from time to time, their pictures stay on the wall, and there's always a place for them at the table.

Two essential truths about the family emerge in this lovely song. First, the family is a natural community, bound by intrinsic spiritual, emotional, and psychological bonds. The family is not created by laws or other conventional institutions, but rather is rooted in the very nature of humankind as the first and most basic human society. As *Gaudium et Spes* puts it, the family is "the primary form of interpersonal communion."[2] Nor is the family merely the invention of a contract between autonomous individuals. The family is not created or sustained by the agreement of its members, but rather exists by the very nature of the procreative and associative relationships without which no family could exist. "Its first task is to live with fidelity the reality of communion in a constant effort to develop an authentic community of persons," explains Pope St. John Paul II in *Familiaris Consortio*.[3]

Second, the family is (or at least should be) the primary witness to the dignity of all persons, regardless of a particular member's abilities, gifts, or contributions. The family is a witness to our mutual dependency on one another, showing us that dignity is not compromised by the need for support and conciliation. "The family ... is a community of persons: of husband and wife, of parents and children, of relatives," continues St. John Paul II. Of course, particular families may be more or less faithful to that witness. But the relative fidelity of a particular family to its mission does not detract from the family's primary purpose of teaching and witnessing to the dignity of all its members, even — if not especially — those members who most need patience and care. "By respecting and fostering personal dignity," explains John Paul II, this care "takes the form of heartfelt acceptance, encounter and dialogue, disinterested availability, generous service and deep solidarity."[4] Moreover, "without love the family is not a community of persons and, in the same way, without love the family cannot live, grow and perfect itself as a community of persons."[5]

Considered together, these two features demonstrate that the family is the most fundamental human association. "In God's plan," teaches John Paul, the family "is the basic cell of society and a subject of rights and duties before the State or any other community."[6] Thus, "the fostering of authentic and mature communion between persons within the family is the first and irreplaceable school of social life, and example and stimulus for the broader community relationships marked by respect, justice, dialogue and love."[7] As noted above, the family is a "natural" society, which means that its existence and structure are given in the very fabric of creation. In the primordial Genesis narrative, woman and man are made for each other and told to be fruitful. In other words, the family of one man and one woman created for the twofold vocation of fellowship and propagation is an essential aspect of creation. As I explain more fully below, the family is the first "necessary" society.

The Family Is the *First* Natural Society

According to the prevailing view in American law and politics, the family has no natural state or structure. Rather, like all other human relationships, the family is mere *convention*; it is a human invention that is as open to alteration or change as any other conventional structure. This is illustrated and instantiated in law by Supreme Court Justice Anthony Kennedy in his opinion in *Obergefell v. Hodges*, the 2015 decision that effectively invalidated states' laws that protected the natural state of marriage. The *Obergefell* decision did not expand marriage to same-sex couples. Rather, it redefined marriage as whatever any two people decide it means. And nothing in *Obergefell* limits this decision to two people. Nor does it limit marriage to two people who are not otherwise already related. If marriage as a natural institution is replaced by a theory of marriage as nothing other than mere convention — the product of the exercise of the purported right to self-definition — there are no coherent arguments against any expression of this convention. Of course, if we already subscribe to the moral anthropology that reduces *all* human associations to negotiated assertions of self-assertive rights, we can't really argue against such a view of "marriage."

In contrast, the Catholic tradition considers the family one of the "three necessary societies," along with the Church and civic community. "Now there are three necessary societies, distinct from one another and yet harmoniously combined by God, into which man is born," explains Pope Pius XI in his 1929 encyclical, *Divini Illius Magistri*. "Two, namely the family and civil society, belong to the natural order; the third, the Church, to the supernatural order."[8] As the first natural society, the family enjoys privilege over civil society, the latter of which exists for the purpose of supporting the family. As Pope Pius explains, "In the first place comes the family, instituted directly by God for its peculiar purpose, the generation and formation of offspring." The family "has priority of nature and therefore of rights over civil society."[9]

The family is the first "helping" society, and therefore is first in the order of subsidiarity. This is a reminder that subsidiarity is not merely about solving problems or addressing issues, but also about proactive formation and education of the person. Every subsidiary structure — from the most basic at the level of the family, to the most remote at the level of international governments and nongovernmental organizations — plays both roles. This is the case whether its participants realize it or not. We cannot overemphasize the importance of a well-formed and well-ordered family, consistent with its natural state. If we lose the family, we lose the very foundation of natural human community.

Commenting on Pope Pius's encyclical, prominent Catholic political philosopher Russell Hittinger observes, "A demise of the necessary societies would mark a social calamity."[10]

Thus we must highlight the vital roles that other helping ("subsidiary") structures should assume in prioritizing and supporting the family. As I discuss more fully below, Catholic social doctrine emphasizes the "subjectivity" of the family: The family exercises moral judgment and makes moral choices, similar to the subjectivity of the individual. Because of this, other structures are often a necessary part of the overall ecology of the family. Whether establishing laws and regulations that support the family, or supplementing the role of families when they are otherwise unable to meet all their obligations, local, state, national, and international governments also play critical roles in the structure and support of the family.

This, again, points to the importance of the proper ordering of the family. Just as the individual human person is properly ordered by and toward rest in God, so too is the family. The family's "first task," in the words of Pope St. John Paul II, "is to live with fidelity the reality of communion in a constant effort to develop an authentic community of persons."[11] This point is illustrated in the bracing accounts of Jesus calling his first apostles in the Gospel of Mark:

> As he passed by the Sea of Galilee, he saw Simon and
> his brother Andrew casting their nets into the sea; they
> were fishermen. Jesus said to them, "Come after me, and
> I will make you fishers of men." Then they abandoned
> their nets and followed him. He walked along a little far-
> ther and saw James, the son of Zebedee, and his brother
> John. They too were in a boat mending their nets. Then
> he called them. So they left their father Zebedee in the
> boat along with the hired men and followed him. (1:16–
> 20; see also 4:18–22)

While the descriptions are short and spare, they show something
deep and profound about the proper ordering of the family. In
both cases, the apostles abandoned their boats and nets to follow
Jesus. And in the case of James and John, we have the additional
detail that they left their father in the boat "mending the nets."
This should not be read as a repudiation of the family. Rather,
the narrative illustrates that the family, including the work of the
family, cannot be ordered properly if it is not ordered toward
Jesus. The family, no less than the individual person, is called
to discipleship. This is what we mean by the subjective nature
of the family. If the family is not properly ordered toward God
through the mediation of the Son, it will not be otherwise properly ordered, regardless of outward appearances.

These texts tell us that the family is *elevated* precisely in being ordered toward and by love of God. One cannot have a proper relationship with any person or group of persons if one's life is
not properly ordered toward God, who alone gives meaning and
purpose to our lives — who alone orders our love toward the
proper objects. Parents can authentically guide their children
in the way of virtue when they direct the family toward love of
God. Siblings find joy not merely in one another's company, but
in the faith that binds them. Children understand their obliga-

tions to their parents only when they have developed the habits and practices of faith — that is, when they leave their nets and follow Jesus. As John Paul II observes:

> Since in God's plan it has been established as an "intimate community of life and love," the family has the mission to become more and more what it is, that is to say, a community of life and love, in an effort that will find fulfillment, as will everything created and redeemed, in the Kingdom of God. Looking at it in such a way as to reach its very roots, we must say that the essence and role of the family are in the final analysis specified by love. Hence the family has the mission to guard, reveal and communicate love, and this is a living reflection of and a real sharing in God's love for humanity and the love of Christ the Lord for the Church His bride.
>
> Every particular task of the family is an expressive and concrete actuation of that fundamental mission.[12]

This elevation of the family as ordered toward love of God is instituted in the fourth commandment, the only of the ten that contains a consequence for its observation: "Honor your father and your mother, that you may have a long life in the land the LORD your God is giving you" (Ex 20:12). A superficial, but not wrong understanding of this commandment is that children are to respect and obey their parents. Certainly, one cannot honor one's parents if one is disobedient to proper instruction or disrespectful at any time. But in the context of Israel's rescue from four hundred years of slavery in Egypt, and its delivery from that bondage by God's agent, Moses, the meaning of the fourth commandment has richer and deeper implications about the role of the family.

At the heart of Israel's bondage in Egypt was the disintegration of the family of Abraham's descendants. Jacob's sons, motivated by jealousy of their brother Joseph, dishonored and deceived their father when they sold Joseph into slavery in Egypt. Of course, Joseph oversaw the growth, storage, and distribution of the crops in Egypt, leading to the brothers' request for mercy and asylum there. After Joseph and his brothers died and a new King of Egypt arose, that asylum became slavery, as recounted in the first chapter of Exodus.

Against this backdrop, the fourth commandment has a deeper meaning than mere respect or obedience to parents. It includes honoring the stories and traditions of the Jews for the purpose of sustaining their history. The people of Israel know who they are because of the education received from their parents about their history and future purpose. Honoring that education is vital to sustaining their very existence as the People of God. Israel is created and sustained by the story. The descendants of Abraham, Isaac, and Jacob continue the story by honoring their parents who tell it, and by communicating it to subsequent generations. They honor the story so that they will live long in the land that God gives them.

Of course, Christians understand that the Old Law is a "disciplinarian," leading to its fulfillment in the life, death, and resurrection of Jesus (see Gal 3:24–25). Yet the commandments are not nullified by this fulfillment. Rather, their whole purpose is revealed. For Christians, obeying the fourth commandment includes telling the story of the Church. This is the continuing way that the Church is sustained over time. Christians, no less than our Jewish parents before us, sustain the story by honoring those who communicate it and, in turn, communicating it to the next generation. This is not for the sake of the story itself, but rather to order our children toward love of God, and to honor our parents for their care in educating us in that love.

"Parental love," observes Pope St. John Paul II, "finds fulfillment in the task of education as it completes and perfects its service of life." This love "is … the animating principle … inspiring and guiding all concrete educational activity, enriching it with the values of kindness, constancy, goodness, service, disinterestedness and self-sacrifice."[13] Thus does Saint Paul admonish parents to bring up their children "with the training and instruction of the Lord" (Eph 6:4), and children to obey their parents, "for this is pleasing to the Lord" (Col 3:20).

Teach Your Children Well

This raises the important issue of *what* we teach our children, a lively public debate in recent years. Battles about curricula in schools, the relative authority of parents to direct or approve of curricula, and the rights of families to supervise their children's education have created a lot of contentious debate. And, of course, ample evidence exists to raise alarms about the drift of education in both public and private contexts. Many Catholic parents have rightly objected to the content of public school curricula, especially as it relates to issues of gender and sexuality. Homeschooling, school vouchers, charter schools, and other alternatives have been on the rise as a response to these problems.

But we Catholics have to ask ourselves hard questions about the moral and political values that we teach our children when we remove them from public schools. We find ourselves in this predicament because of an education in liberal, self-actualizing individualism. If we find an educational alternative that provides our children with the same formation in individualism and voluntaristic moral theory as they get in the public schools, how is this really an alternative? The family is the first teacher. But we Catholics must be able to distinguish the basic moral values of modern liberalism from the classic notions of virtue rooted in the Catholic theological tradition. Otherwise, we cannot lay a truly Catholic educational foundation. We cannot simultaneously object to the inevitable result of an education in liberal individualism while teaching the same moral language to our children, but with a veneer of the *Catechism* painted over it. Education is the family's prerogative, but we must pay attention to what we are instilling: Is it discipleship to Christ or loyalty to American individualism?

The answer is crucial because the broader society has an interest in a proper definition of the family, and institutional support of it. Our witness to the primacy of a Christian understanding of the family is not limited to the education of our children. In our expressions of political opinions and choices of public policy options, do we advocate a public witness for the family? Or do we tend to privatize the family in the same way that we tend to privatize individual morality? In other words, are our commitments to public and political theories about the family formed by partisan political loyalty or by the full implications of the family as the first subsidiary institution within the larger framework of public and political life? We cannot coherently advocate for the family as a strong example of social solidarity while supporting individualist or libertarian political theories that undermine that advocacy.

This raises important questions about how we vote to collect and spend public resources, and for whom we vote to make policy about the use of those resources. The family is the "first and vital cell of society," explains John Paul II.[14] "The family has vital and organic links with society," he continues. "It is from the family that citizens come to birth and it is within the family that they find the first school of the social virtues that are the animating principle of the existence and development of society itself."[15] Thus society at large — not only Catholic Christians — has a stake in the well-being and proper ordering of the family. "The family is by nature and vocation open to other families and to society." Thus it has a necessary "social role."[16]

This is not to say that it is the mandate of the family to "make society better." We order our family according to the truth of its natural structure, not to affect society one way or the other. The mandate of the family is to teach, model, and support virtues consistent with the Gospel. But if all families are structured in a truthful way, the social implications will be positive. "The very experience of communion and sharing that should characterize the family's daily life represents its first and fundamental contribution to society," explains John Paul II. "Thus the fostering of authentic and mature communion between persons within the family is the first and irreplaceable school of social life, an example and stimulus for the broader community relationships marked by respect, justice, dialogue and love."[17]

And because we are charged with ordering our lives in accord with the Gospel, it is only natural for us to advocate policies, programs, and civic structures that are consistent with that order. Indeed, the social subjectivity of the family as the first subsidiary structure necessarily implies that the broader society must defer to the priority of the family. This includes legal and regulatory structures that acknowledge and support the integrity of the family and its precedence in social consideration. "Therefore, neither society nor the State may absorb, substitute or reduce the social dimension of the family; rather, they must honor it, recognize it, respect it and promote it according to the principle of subsidiarity."[18] The family is the first "helping" society; all other social structures are ordered toward the well-being of the family.

This mandate must include a host of policies that support rather than replace the family. Many of these policies will not fit with either of the two major political parties in the United States. The issues that I discuss below will be a test of whether our policy preferences are more informed by Catholic moral reflection or partisan loyalty. The answers I suggest are not a middle way between the left and right wings of American liberalism. Rather, they are rooted in a fundamental commitment to the four pillars of Catholic social doctrine, and the policy implications that flow from them.

The remainder of this chapter will discuss these policies under three considerations:

1. Rethinking abortion language
2. Free or subsidized birth
3. Paid parental leave

Rethinking Abortion Language

On June 24, 2022, the United States Supreme Court handed down one of the most momentous decisions in its history in the case of *Dobbs v. Jackson Women's Health*. In *Dobbs* the Court overruled two of its most notorious decisions, *Roe v. Wade* (1973) and *Planned Parenthood of Southeastern Pennsylvania v. Casey* (1993). While the implications are enormous, the court's holding is rather simple. The Constitution of the United States does not prohibit individual states from proscribing or otherwise restricting access to abortion. "The Constitution does not prohibit the citizens of each State from regulating or prohibiting abortion," wrote Associate Justice Samuel Alito for the 6–3 majority. But, of course, *Dobbs* did not end the political or legal debate about the legality of abortion. Rather, it shifted the debate to the fifty states, where it had been taking place before *Roe*. *Dobbs* did not end the war to defend unborn human life, but rather moved the battles to multiple fronts.

In response to *Dobbs*, both pro-life and pro-abortion advocates have been hard at work pressing their representatives to pass abortion-related legislation, or introducing ballot referenda. Individual states have passed laws and regulations related to abortion access, ranging from near-total bans on abortion on the one hand, to protecting abortion on demand up to and even after birth. And as the laws have been passed, new waves of litigation have arisen across the country, testing the limits of various statutes and regulations against both state constitutions and federal civil laws that might be read as having implications for abortion access. As noted above, *Dobbs* did not end the war but rather multiplied the legislative and litigation battles.

Important as legislative initiatives are, we must think about abortion less as a legal or political issue than as a moral one. And in prioritizing the moral case against abortion, we must rethink the language we use. Catholics cannot win the moral case against abortion if we use a language that already surrenders the moral case to the other side. By accepting the moral anthropology in which a language of individual rights is rooted, we might be conceding the abortion argument before it even begins. We cannot make a coherent case against abortion if we endorse and use a moral language that absolutizes the right to abortion. Put simply, we must learn how to remove the abortion debate from the language of individual rights claims. If we do not do this, we will lose the moral argument. And if we lose the moral argument, we will lose the legal, regulatory, and public policy arguments as well. The loss may be gradual, but it will be certain.

Of course, one might argue that I am ignoring something even more basic than the language we use to argue about abortion. Conversion to the full truth of the Gospel is a more fundamental solution to any social problem, abortion included. This objection is well taken, but only to a point. A very significant percentage of tireless opponents of abortion, including those on the front lines of pro-life advocacy, are strongly committed Catholic and Evangelical Christians. Their motives and pure devotion are heartfelt, but most of them still use the language of individual rights claims in articulating their defense of the life of the unborn child. I admire and respect the authenticity of people who devote such energy to protecting unborn life. But if we are using moral language that concedes abortion as a clash of rights, we will always lose the argument.

As I explained in chapter 1, rights language is rooted in a moral theory by which we live in a war of every person against every person. The word *rights* in this moral theory demonstrates the inherent alienation of every person from every person. Rather than communicate and encourage the natural solidarity of all human persons, rights language is born from a theory in which we are all enemies, and it perpetuates that falsehood.

Applied to abortion, this has two related implications. First, by casting abortion in terms of individual rights (including the purported right of the unborn child), we perpetuate the lie that the unborn child and mother are rivals against one another, with competing claims of rights. Rather than seeing the child and mother as the most intimate form of human community, we see them as the most fundamental enemies.

The second problem with casting abortion as a clash of the rights of the mother against the rights of the child is that we have no rational way to adjudicate whose claims prevail in the event of a perceived or asserted conflict. Or worse, the weight of argument favors the "right" of the mother to rid herself of the intrusive assertions of the rights of the child. When there are no adjudicating principles between competing and incompatible claims of rights, the resolution of those conflicts will fall to something else, such as individual power or mere democratic whim. Even legislative victories protecting the lives of unborn children are built upon a fragile foundation, subject to collapse at the change of the political wind.

As I noted in chapter 3, I realize that even Church documents utilize a kind of rights language. But that language does not express assertions of competing rights, but rather the protections and immunities that are a necessary corollary of the natural dignity of the human person. But that is not what the average American means by *rights*, nor is it how most American Catholics understand assertions of rights. We have been raised in a moral and political climate, from the very foundation of the United States, that we are bearers of claims against one another as autonomous individual rights bearers. While I understand that it is a major undertaking, requiring a good deal of reorienting our moral language, we would do better to jettison rights language altogether, and replace it with the language of Catholic social doctrine, built upon the fourfold foundation of dignity, solidarity, subsidiarity, and common good.

The tension I am describing is illustrated in the most important abortion-related encyclical of Pope St. John Paul II, *Evangelium Vitae*. While John Paul articulates a defense of unborn life in terms of the "right" to life (understood, again, as rooted in human dignity and community, not individualist autonomy), he implicitly accounts for the danger of using the language of rights because of the way it is almost universally understood in modern liberal societies. He turns his attention to various attacks on human life in its earliest stage. Once considered crimes, these attacks now "assume the nature of 'rights,' to the point that the State is called upon to give them legal recognition and to make them available through the free services of health-care personnel," John Paul laments.[19] Even worse, he continues, "those attacks are carried out in the very heart of and with the complicity of the family — the family which by its nature is called to be the 'sanctuary of life.'"[20]

Again, when Pope John Paul uses the language of rights (in this and other encyclicals), he obviously uses that language as an expression of the necessary implications of human dignity and solidarity. And if this was the universally recognized meaning of *rights*, the language could be used without concern. But, as the pope himself illustrates, this is *not* how most people understand rights. Instead, rights are understood precisely in the way that I have described them throughout this book, as competing claims of power by autonomous, isolated, and "naturally" atomistic individuals. Indeed, John Paul observes that the background of the crisis he describes is a "profound crisis of culture, which generates skepticism in relation to the very foundations of knowledge and ethics, and which makes it increasingly difficult to grasp clearly the meaning of what man is, the meaning of his rights and his duties."[21] This is why he puts "rights" in scare quotes in the passage cited above, to account for what once were considered crimes. But the meaning in the scare quotes is the meaning embraced by the vast majority of Americans, including the majority of American Catholics.

We can only offer a coherent and intelligible account for the protection of unborn life if we recover a moral language that begins with the dignity of all human beings as created in the image and likeness of God. Moreover, we must reiterate the natural solidarity and the subsidiary nature of the human person. This implies both that we are united as participants in the same shared nature and that we are dependent upon one another as an essential aspect of our being. The moral case against abortion cannot be won using the language of individual rights. On the contrary, using that language is the guarantee that it will be lost — indeed, that it is already lost.

And our use of this language distorts our perception and support of other policy options, including those related to the care and nurture of expectant mothers and newborn infants.

Free or Subsidized Birth

It hardly needs to be noted that the foundation of the Catholic theology of the family is openness to new life. The twofold purpose of marriage is the unity of the couple and the procreation of children. "The transmission of human life is a most serious role in which married people collaborate freely and responsibly with God the Creator," explained Pope St. Paul VI in *Humanae Vitae*.[22] "By their very nature," adds *Gaudium et Spes*, "the institution of matrimony itself and conjugal love are ordained for the procreation and education of children, and find in them their ultimate crown."[23] If you are reading this book, you are probably already committed to the truth of the Church's teaching on procreation, so I will not go into detail about it here. Rather, I will suggest that this moral mandate to be open to children necessarily suggests the need for strong public policies that favor and support begetting and raising children. This includes sharing the economic costs and easing the economic burdens of having children.

In July 2022, shortly after the overruling of *Roe v. Wade* by *Dobbs v. Jackson Women's Health Organization*, Elizabeth Breunig published an essay in *The Atlantic*, entitled "Make Birth Free: It's Time the Pro-life Movement Chose Life."[24] In January 2023, Catherine Glenn Foster, president of Americans United for Life, and Kristen Day, executive director of Democrats for Life of America, posted a white paper entitled *Make Birth Free: A Vision for Congress to Empower American Mothers, Families, and Communities*.[25] Both documents lay out a compelling case for universal, federally funded pregnancy, childbirth, and postpartum care. In addition to the specifics of the proposals, they are also examples of how some social issues simply do not fit the traditional partisan divide in America's two-party system. The proposal for universal health care for pregnancy, childbirth, and postpartum care falls squarely within the four pillars of Catholic social doctrine, which ought to be our starting point for policy considerations.

At the outset, I want to deflect an obvious objection: None of the authors of these proposals (or the many commentators supporting and tweaking their suggestions) believe that such a large-scale government program would be "free." Indeed, they acknowledge the considerable cost of such a program, and discuss various methods of collecting and administering tax funds that would finance free birth. "Make birth free" is a rhetorical device to communicate a policy proposal that would spread the cost of carrying and delivering a child across an entire taxpaying population, whether on a state or federal level. "Free birth" is a cipher for "shared cost of birth." But the rationale for the policy proposal is that the benefit of sharing the expense of birth will far outweigh the social costs of our current system.

Among peer high-income countries, the United States ranks very poorly for infant and birth-related maternal mortality.[26] In 2020, the infant mortality rate in the United States was 5.4 deaths per one thousand live births.[27] Norway, by contrast, has the lowest rate at 1.6 deaths per thousand live births. The maternal mortality rates are just as disturbing. In 2020, the maternal mortality rate in the United States was almost twenty-four per one hundred thousand live births, more than triple the rate in most other developed peer countries — even though the United States spends two to four times as much on health care as the same peer countries. For the United States, the question is not the amount that we spend on health care, but how we spend it. Encouraging and supplementing healthy births and perinatal care — and redirecting health care dollars toward that care — would almost certainly be a more efficient way of spending health care dollars. Certainly, it would be more in accord with the principles of Catholic social doctrine.

Solely from the standpoint of Catholic moral theology, any policies that encourage life should be presumptively favorable, even if the details of specific programs are open to prudential judgment and discussion. A Catholic conversation for such a program should default to favoring policies and programs that encourage healthy pregnancy and childbirth, and that remove financial burdens. Care must be taken in both the way revenue is raised and how assets are disbursed. Basic principles of efficiency, fairness, and equity must be taken into consideration. And, like all considerations of subsidiary structures, the moral agency of parents and family must be supported, not subsumed. But even so, the discussion should be had in the context of the fourfold doctrines of dignity, solidarity, subsidiarity, and common good, not the twofold ideologies of American partisan politics.

Moreover, if we are sincerely committed to encouraging procreation as a social good, we should recognize that economic considerations are not the primary concern. Of course, economic impacts are important, especially as the cost of a free birth program will have ripple effects across the economy. It would be irresponsible not to take other costs into consideration. But as Catholic Christians, committed to the dignity of the human person, solidarity, subsidiarity, and the common good, we must not reduce suggestions like free birth to mere economic matters. Nor should we begin the discussion with economic considerations and mold the policy accordingly. Rather, we must begin with our commitment to human life as a social good, and work to make the economics fit that commitment. We must resist the contemporary libertarian temptation to start every policy discussion with dollars and cents. We are Catholics. And even if, in good faith, we might determine that the costs of such a program outweigh its benefits, we begin with Catholic principles of social doctrine, not libertarian economic considerations.

Catherine Foster and Kristen Day point out that even with high-quality, employer-based health insurance, the out-of-pocket cost for a family to bear a child averages from three thousand to five thousand dollars.[28] And that is assuming no medical complications for mother or developing child. Many well-meaning couples who desire to have children simply do not have the means to bear this cost. If the newborn baby requires neonatal intensive care, out-of-pocket expenses for families often exceed ten thousand dollars.[29] Elizabeth Breunig reports specific examples of such costs, reaching as much as twenty-four thousand dollars for a high-risk delivery in Indiana. In Colorado, a hospital billed the mother fourteen thousand dollars for a routine delivery, of which the mother was on the hook for five thousand dollars out of pocket.[30] These examples are replicated throughout the United States. According to Foster and Day, "Maternity care in the United States is uniquely expensive." In other developed countries, the out-of-pocket cost of comprehensive maternity and birth is either free or practically free. Citing Ireland and Finland as examples, Foster and Day point out that infant mortality rates are also lower where comprehensive maternity care is provided through public funds.

Day and Foster calculate that, given the average cost of childbirth in the United States, "the approximately 3.6 million annual births ... would cost about $68 billion." They point out that 42 percent of live births are already covered for low-income families through Medicaid, leaving about $39.5 billion that would be covered by new spending, either on the state or federal level.[31] This is less than the $54 billion of aid sent to Ukraine in 2022 alone, just to cite one comparative example.[32] Day and Foster go into further details about perverse economic incentives and disincentives that could be alleviated by free birth.[33] While important, these are secondary to the moral case for free birth.[34] Moreover, as noted above, for the United States, the problem in health care spending is inefficiency, not amount. Preventive health care and health care maintenance are more efficient than emergent care and treatment of preventable disease and injury.

Perhaps nothing indicates the inherent dignity of the human person (including the unborn and their parents) more than a social program that is welcoming and encouraging of the proliferation of humans. Potential parents should not be dissuaded from having children because of the perceived cost or stigma of childbearing. Rather, Catholic-informed social policy advocacy should send every available signal that children are welcome and families who have children are valued. We cannot simultaneously affirm the dignity of the human person while advocating for social policies that discourage their birth or hinder the health of newborns or their mothers. Human dignity does not imply mere tolerance of new life, but rather proactive encouragement and support. Yes, we must count the cost. But we should make the cost fit the policy, not vice versa.

What does the idea of highly subsidized or free birth mean for the Catholic principle of solidarity? If we take seriously the essential social nature of the human person, along with its implication that we are born to care for one another, then we must share the cost of the most basic part of human development — conception and birth. Having children, whether the cost is borne solely by the family or spread over the entire population, is not a "private" event. On the contrary, hardly anything is more "social" than adding another person to society. The doctrine of solidarity suggests a very strong presumption that the cost of adding that person should be shared by all as a sign of welcoming hospitality, the essence of solidarity. If we want houses with crowded tables — as we should — we must joyfully share the cost of providing them.

This is not to suggest that we encourage irresponsible choices by couples who may not be able to bear the nonfinancial burdens of childbirth. Indeed, the central document of Catholic teaching on childbirth, *Humanae Vitae*, contemplates the regulation of childbirth (by natural means, of course) for serious reasons. "With regard to physical, economic, psychological and social conditions, responsible parenthood is exercised by those who prudently and generously decide to have more children, and by those who, for serious reasons and with due respect to moral precepts, decide not to have additional children for either a certain or an indefinite period of time."[35] To advocate for free childbirth is not to advocate for irresponsible parenting. The same considerations that apply to responsible planning for families should pertain across the spectrum of society. But within those considerations, the doctrine of solidarity suggests that we share the joy and burden of new life when it is otherwise appropriate for families to grow.

Of course, the commitment to solidarity must be consistent with principles of subsidiarity. But remember that *subsidiarity* is not simply a libertarian term for smaller government; it comes from the Latin word for "help," "assist," or "aid." Subsidiary structures are helping structures, not necessarily small or local. The presumption is that people, including people in families, are dependent upon others for their well-being. Subsidiarity already assumes solidarity, or else it makes no sense. To be sure, Catholic teaching emphasizes that the "helping" structure should be as small, local, and immediate as is consistent with its effectiveness. If smaller is better, smaller is mandatory.

Subsidiarity is not a prohibition of social programs, however, but a means of ordering them, according to which social help is administered on the proper level. The question is not whether new parents require assistance in bearing and welcoming children. Of course they do! As Alasdair MacIntyre has noted, "We human beings are vulnerable to many kinds of affliction. ... How we cope is only in small part up to us. It is most often to others that we owe our survival, let alone our flourishing. ... This dependence on particular others for protection and sustenance is most obvious in early childhood and in old age."[36]

Subsidiarity does not ask whether help should be given, but rather what form that assistance should take, consistent with dignity and moral agency. Moral agents are not wholly immune from social contingencies, though we must not replace moral agency with bureaucratic management. A comprehensive program for free birth might be better administered under programs in individual states through existing Medicaid and other social welfare programs. Or it may be that the most efficient administration of a free birth program would be through something like the federal Medicare program. In both cases, the bureaucratic structure is already in place. Another possibility is to offset the out-of-pocket expense of childbirth through tax credits, or even direct cash transfers. Yet another option might be for state and federal policy to incentivize private insurers and employers to provide comprehensive free birth, or to disincentivize out-of-pocket expenses such as deductibles and copays.

People of good will might disagree about the most efficient means of implementing programs, and good cases may be made for these or other proposals. In any event, the doctrine of subsidiarity does not suggest *whether* free birth is good social policy, but rather how that social policy should be implemented. Help is required. The policy question is where and how that help is most appropriately administered while preserving the moral agency of the family. These are not "conservative" or "liberal" proposals. They are not "Republican" or "Democrat." Rather, they are proposals rooted in fourfold Catholic social doctrine. This doctrine resists identification with any brand of liberal politics because it is rooted in the moral anthropology of Catholic Christianity, not liberal political theory.

Paid Parental Leave?

Closely related to the social good of free childbirth is a generous policy of paid parental leave. The moral arguments supporting prenatal care and subsidized birth apply to sharing the cost of very early childhood development and parental transition. The question is not whether parents with newborns need help, but rather what kind of help they need and how it is best administered. And, again, the solution is not founded in libertarian economics or individualist moral philosophy, but rather in dignity, solidarity, subsidiarity, and the common good.

As with the cost of childbirth, the United States is an outlier when it comes to providing for federally assisted paid parental leave. Some individual states have moderate paid leave programs. And many private companies have paid leave benefits, often tiered by partial pay through a certain number of weeks, followed by an option for unpaid leave for an additional number of weeks. Sadly, as some readers of this book may have experienced, Catholic institutions, including some Catholic dioceses and archdioceses, provide less generous paid leave than similarly sized or situated secular businesses or organizations. And, while the federal Family and Medical Leave Act requires some employers to provide twelve weeks of *unpaid* leave, the United States is one of very few developed countries with no national paid maternity or other paid family leave programs or mandates.

Again, the principles of dignity, solidarity, subsidiarity, and the common good, rather than the ideologies of partisan politics, ought to form our thinking about the propriety, in principle, of state or federally mandated paid maternal or family leave, especially related to newborns and infants. These policies must take into consideration various incentives and disincentives. For example, the principle of subsidiarity suggests that families who have the independent financial means to care for young children without public assistance should be incentivized to do so. And while social policy should not discourage two-income families, neither should it penalize families who make the choice to forego an income from one parent for the sake of staying at home with young children. We should stigmatize neither families for whom two incomes are necessary, nor those who subordinate financial considerations to nurturing children. Finding the proper balance in these considerations is not an easy task. But our discussion of them should begin with the presumption that we all have a stake in, and thus responsibility for, policies and programs that attempt to address various legitimate options. And we must be willing to direct policy toward the solutions most in accord with the principles of Catholic social doctrine.

In the case of paid or subsidized family leave, the principles of solidarity and subsidiarity are our primary guides. Solidarity applies to families no less than to individuals. Families are not insular. The relative health and well-being of any family impacts others. While charity rather than "family interest" should be our primary motivation for the care of other families, we cannot ignore the social impact that dysfunctional families have on the larger social fabric. Solidarity is not an aspiration; it is a reality. The question for social policy is how solidarity challenges us to make public choices consistent with the inseparable web of social relationships. Similarly, the doctrine of subsidiarity requires us to ask what level of help for families is consistent with moral agency. As I noted in chapter 3, the measure of subsidiarity is not size or proximity, but the level of help that is consistent with the integrity of the moral agent. This applies to the subjective agency of the family no less than to agency of the individual person.

Various proposals can be considered. Perhaps the most obvious is to modify the federal Family and Medical Leave Act (or similar state programs) to require large companies to provide paid parental leave. Any such laws or regulations should continue to take into account the relative size of the company and other considerations that make such a mandate more or less feasible. Requiring employers to provide paid leave (rather than wealth-shifting programs) is probably most consistent with the principle of subsidiarity. When paid family leave can be borne by a direct employer, it can be administered more efficiently than larger wealth transfer programs administered by state or federal treasuries. Of course, laws and regulations that encourage (or require) such programs might be necessary. But the closer to the employer and employee that such programs are, the more efficiently they may be administered. Companies would be given the flexibility to design programs that are most consistent with the good of the family balanced with fairness to other employees and the sustainability of the company, so long as they comport with minimum standards of paid leave.

As another option, expanded child tax credits for young children would make it easier for one parent to stay home with infants and young children. Such credits should be indexed to average family wages and other calculations that take into consideration the opportunity cost of staying home versus going back to work outside the home. Such a calculation may consider the equivalent wage value of homemaking, including the whole suite of services that are provided by stay-at-home parents. For example, we could conceive of a more generous tax credit program for parents who choose to stay at home versus those who choose paid childcare. We can respect both choices while favoring one over the other.

If direct aid rather than tax credits is a more efficient means of accomplishing the same social goals, that also should be considered. We must not shy away from discussion of things like guaranteed minimum income programs simply because they are generally associated with the "wrong" political party or ideology. By no means am I suggesting that such direct transfers should immediately be implemented, if implemented at all. I am suggesting, however, that the four pillars of Catholic social doctrine set out the perimeters for the legitimacy of discussing such programs, especially for families with young children in the most formative years. If we take the moral theology of the Church seriously, we cannot reject such a discussion simply because it does (or does not) comport with the fiscal or economic policy of one or the other political party.

Put another way, the standard we should use to measure the propriety of such programs should be the fourfold principles of

Catholic social doctrine, rather than the twofold constrictions of American partisan politics. If we cannot divorce ourselves from the default mentality of American partisanship and wholly embrace Catholic moral principles, we cannot have an authentic discussion of these and other political, economic, social, and civic matters. Nor can we present a coherent witness against the moral anthropology that informs the social maladies that devalue children, parenthood, and traditional families.

Prudence Must Guide Policy Choices

In closing this chapter, I want to emphasize again that a broad range of legitimate options are available in a discussion about practical laws, regulations, and institutions for the social support of the family. Within the basic framework of the four pillars of Catholic social doctrine, there may be many feasible, good-faith alternative arguments. I am not suggesting that any particular way of expressing the proper subsidiary structures is the correct one.

Rather, I am calling for us Catholics to reorient ourselves so that the discussion is sustained in a coherent Catholic understanding of the nature of the human person. The regnant structure of liberal individualism that characterizes both major political parties in the United States *cannot* offer solutions consistent with the entire range of social doctrine because it begins with a moral anthropology that expressly rejects that doctrine. One cannot simultaneously affirm the solidarity of all human persons and the individualism of modern liberalism. If one affirms the latter, one cannot frame a coherent argument for the natural structure of the family. Nor, if we embrace that individualist morality, can we articulate an intelligible argument for subsidiary structures to support the family. If we accede to the ideology of liberalism, we underwrite the very moral anthropology that undermines Catholic morality.

Chapter 5
Work: Where Dignity and Solidarity Meet

Work and the worker are at the very heart of Catholic social doctrine. This is why Pope Leo XIII began his 1891 encyclical *Rerum Novarum* with a consideration of the challenges of work in the modern industrial economy. Granted, the theological principles that have been applied to develop the Church's teaching on labor and the economy are not new. But beginning in the late nineteenth century, the Church began to think about the economy of labor in the context of the moral tradition of the Church. Catholic social doctrine developed as a distinct discipline within the scope of Catholic moral theology to address the nature of work, the relationship of labor to capital, and the broader question of a modern industrial economy as it arose in the second half of the nineteenth century.

By the time Pope Leo promulgated *Rerum Novarum*, Western economies had undergone revolutionary changes in the nature of labor and the relationship of the worker to his work. Before the industrial revolution, most workers made their own livings through agriculture or small, self-sufficient manufacturing concerns. From planting to cultivation to carrying grain or produce to market, farms were small family businesses. The farmer was involved in every aspect of the work and oversaw the growth of his own crops or livestock. For tradesmen, the situation was similar. Whether alone, with a few employees, or in a workers' cooperative, the typical worker was involved in the entire creation of the goods he grew or sold, from gathering of raw materials, to forging or fabricating of parts, to assembly or manufacture, to marketing. Of course, these are broad generalities, for which there were significant exceptions. But by and large, before the Industrial Revolution, farmers, laborers, and tradesmen were involved in every aspect of their work, maintaining their own agency over the process and product of their labor. This changed radically and quickly with the Industrial Revolution, which had at least three effects for the worker.

First, the modern industrial economy removed the worker from his own farm or shop to a manufacturing or assembly plant that was owned by someone else, who supplied the raw materials or component parts for the product being made. The source of the "capital" was different from the source of the work.

Second, the laborer no longer maintained his own agency over the entire production of the goods to be made and sold. Rather, as in an assembly line, he might be involved in only a small part of the manufacture or assembly. Indeed, in many cases, he might contribute to a component part of some machine or larger product of which he was not even aware. In other words, the worker was separated from the work of his hands as the process of manufacturing and assembly was modernized and industrialized.

Third, the worker no longer received direct payment from the sale of his finished goods or products. Rather, he was now paid a salary by the owner of the factory and assembly line. His work became another in a list of "commodities" that contributed to the final product to be sold by someone else. He sold his labor, not his product. This raised important questions about the fairness of salaries or wages, and the rise of the concept of "profit." If the labor is a commodity, is the laborer merely a commodity, too? If the product is sold for a price that is greater than the cost of producing it (including the cost of labor), who owns the difference? Should it be the worker, without whom the product could not have been manufactured or assembled? Or should it be the capitalist, without whom the factory, material, and means of production could not be supplied? Whose risk in the enterprise should be more highly regarded and rewarded?

The rapid pace of the Industrial Revolution outpaced comprehensive answers to these questions. And many proposed answers involved the rejection of essential aspects of Catholic moral teaching. Consider Marxism, for example, which became the prevailing philosophical response in the nineteenth century. The Industrial Revolution was closely followed by a labor revolution. But the labor revolution was rooted in an atheistic and materialistic understanding of the nature of man and morality, which involved the rejection of the theological foundation of Catholic moral theology. The Marxist critique of the modern labor economy had (and has) legitimate aspects, especially regarding the alienation of the worker from his work, just wages, and the proper distribution of profit. We cannot ignore these critiques simply because we cannot accept Marxism's proposed resolutions, which also go against the principles of Catholic social doctrine.

Within this context, and with these problems in mind, in 1891, Pope Leo XIII wrote in *Rerum Novarum* that the "spirit of revolutionary change" of the 1800s had "made its influence felt in the ... sphere of practical economics." This revolutionary spirit had ushered in a crisis in moral consideration. "The elements of the conflict," the pope wrote, included "the vast expansion of industrial pursuits and the marvelous discoveries of science; ... the changed relations between masters and workmen; ... the enormous fortunes of some few individuals, and the utter poverty of the masses; [and] the increased self-reliance and closer mutual combination of the working classes."[1]

Thus the pope continued:

> We thought it expedient now to speak on the condition of the working classes. It is a subject on which We have already touched more than once, incidentally. But in the present letter, the responsibility of the apostolic office urges Us to treat the question of set purpose and in detail, in order that no misapprehension may exist as to the principles which truth and justice dictate for its settlement.[2]

Thus Leo ushered in a new body of theological reflection on the nature of work and the worker that developed through the twentieth and twenty-first centuries. In 1981, Pope St. John Paul II wrote the encyclical *Laborem Exercens*,[3] which was promulgated to celebrate the ninetieth anniversary of *Rerum Novarum*. John Paul's purpose was "to call attention to the dignity and rights of those who work, to condemn situations in which that dignity and those rights are violated, and to help to guide the above-mentioned changes so as to ensure authentic progress by man and society."[4] These and related matters are the concern of this chapter.

Work Is Natural and Essential to the Human Person

In our consideration of work, we turn once again to the opening chapters of the Book of Genesis, where our very first impression of God is that he is a Creator. Indeed, the first account even refers to his creativity as "work," telling us that God rested from his work on the seventh day. "On the seventh day God completed the work he had been doing; he rested on the seventh day from all the work he had undertaken. ... He rested from all the work he had done in creation" (Gn 2:2, 3b). Creative work is "natural" to God. Because the human person is made in the image and likeness of God, man is also ordered in his essential nature to work.

Genesis gives us additional information about work as natural to the human person. In the second creation account, after God had "made the earth and the heavens," God did not yet cause it to rain, and thus no plants or grass had sprouted. Why? Because "there was no man to till the ground" (Gn 2:4–5). So God created the human person as caretaker of the soil. After man was created, "God then took the man and settled him the garden of Eden, to cultivate and care for it" (Gn 2:15). This shows us both the ordered design of creation and man's participative role in it.

We see an example of this when God brings all the nonhuman animals to the man for him to name. God both permits and instructs the human person to share in God's creative activity. The human person was expressly created for the purpose of working with the earth that God had created. Another way of saying this is that man was made to *participate* in God's creation. Without God's creative work, of course, no created thing exists, yet God gave the human person the role of tending to his creation. Work is essential to the nature of the human person. Pope St. John Paul II observes that "work is a fundamental dimension of human existence on earth." The image of God is reflected "partly through the mandate ... to subdue ... the earth," he continues. "In carrying out this mandate, ... every human being reflects the very action of the Creator of the universe."[5]

As discussed in chapter 2, being made in the image and likeness of God is the foundation of the unique dignity of the human person among all God's creatures. Because work is natural to the human person — indeed, it is part of the very reason for our existence — work itself has inherent dignity. This dignity is expressed in the very ability of man to work, and thus to contribute to his own personal development. As I discuss more fully below, this is an aspect of the "subjective" nature of work, as compared to its "objective" nature. For now, it is enough to note that work, as an intended aspect of the natural dignity of the human person, is itself imbued with dignity.

But perhaps you think, "My work is not very dignified, nor is much of the work that I observe around me." And it is true that for many people, work is a tedious, arduous grind rather than a dignified activity. This does not refute the natural, inherent dignity of work, however. Rather, the drudgery of work is yet another result of the Fall of the human person. The essence of the Fall is the rejection of God as man's final end. Since this most fundamental relationship is now disordered, it naturally follows that all other aspects of human life are also disordered. This includes work and our relationship to work.

Another name for this disorder is *alienation*. When we alienate ourselves from God, we are alienated from every other good that is natural to the human person, including work. A theology of work must begin with this fundamental problem of alienation. Indeed, alienation is at the heart of the Marxist critique of the industrialized economy. Unfortunately, Marx was wrong about both the causes and remedies for this alienation, a point that is explored more fully below.

The specific expression of our alienation from work after the Fall is illustrated in the third chapter of Genesis. "Cursed be the ground because of you!" God declares. "In toil you shall eat its yield all the days of your life. Thorns and thistles shall it bring forth for you. ... By the sweat of your brow you shall eat bread" (Gn 3:17–19a). Similarly, after Cain slays Abel in chapter four of Genesis, God tells Cain, "If you till the ground, it shall no longer give you its produce" (Gn 4:12). Thus Cain was alienated from his proper and natural end of cultivating the earth and forced to wander as an alien in the land.

Alienation from work is a common experience of many people (even those who have not killed a sibling). But, like all aspects of human life, God has redeemed work in the life, death, and resurrection of Christ. This means that God has given us a renewed understanding of the nature and purpose of work, as well as the theological resources to articulate a revival of the dignity of all work. In the context of our redemption in Christ, even work that does not seem to be very dignified can be ordered toward its proper ends and purposes, thus restoring its dignity.

The Dignity of Work

In his 1901 memoir, *Up from Slavery*, Booker T. Washington recounts his role in the founding and growth of what is now known as Tuskegee University in Alabama. Tuskegee was one of many secondary schools, colleges, and universities that were founded after the abolition of slavery. Their purposes were to educate and provide agricultural, technical, and mechanical training for freed slaves and their descendants, so that they could support themselves and contribute to the economy. When Washington, the son of a slave, was appointed the first president of Tuskegee in 1881, the school consisted of a single room in a church building. In 1882, Washington purchased a former plantation, which became the permanent site of the university.

Over the next several years, the students at Tuskegee literally built the campus by making the bricks and erecting the buildings in which they were to live and study. They did this at the same time that they were cultivating the farmland of the plantation to support themselves and the school, and engaging in an academic curriculum. Washington's purpose in doing this was not simply to teach the students construction and carpentry skills on the fly, though that was one happy result. More importantly, he intended to instill in these early generations of freed slaves the nature, purpose, and dignity of work. In doing the work themselves, he observed, the students "would be taught to see not only utility in labor, but beauty and dignity; would be taught, in fact, how to lift labor up from mere drudgery and toil, and would learn to love work for its own sake."[6]

Washington was applying a lesson he had learned from his own student days at Hampton Institute, another of the early schools for freed slaves, when he was asked to assist in cleaning the buildings in preparation for the start of the school year. He agreed to the work, but only because it was "a chance to secure a credit in the treasurer's office"[7] to help with his tuition. When Washington arrived at Hampton for the job, he was amazed to find the principal of the school, Mary F. Mackie, working alongside the young students, "cleaning windows, dusting rooms, putting beds in order, and what not."[8] He marveled that Mackie, "a member of one of the oldest and most cultured families of the North. … took the greatest satisfaction" in scrubbing every windowpane until it was perfectly clean.[9] He explained later, "It was hard for me at this time to understand how a woman of her education and social standing could take such delight in performing such service."[10] But the lesson took. "Ever since then I have had no patience with any school for my race in the South which did not teach its students the dignity of labor."[11]

Years later, when he enlisted the students to build the campus at Tuskegee, Washington knew that he was sacrificing the efficiency and fine finish that professional architects and skilled bricklayers and carpenters would have brought to the project. But he considered the benefit to the students of doing the work worth the relative lack of professional quality. Applying the lesson he had learned from "Miss Mackie" at Hampton, Washington observed that "the teaching of civilization, self-help, and self-reliance, the erection of the buildings by the students themselves would more than compensate for any lack of comfort or fine finish."[12] More than erecting the buildings, the students were learning firsthand how labor instills dignity in the worker. Indeed, I think that Washington would say that the lessons were more important and consequential than the buildings.

I do have one minor quibble with the way Washington describes the work that his Tuskegee students performed. Washington writes that he wanted his students "to love work for its own sake."[13] In a highly qualified sense, this is a proper — albeit incomplete — description of work. Certainly, it is good and proper to take satisfaction in performing work well. The emotional or psychological satisfaction that comes from completing a task can be an example of loving work for its own sake. Enjoying one's work, including the product of the labor, is better than not enjoying it. But this is an incomplete account of the purpose of work, even work that is satisfying and enjoyable. In fact, devotion to work can interfere with an understanding of the higher end of work.

But Washington himself understood this. And his fuller explanation moves us toward an account of work that we Catholics can fully embrace. As he worked his way through Hampton to pay his tuition, he learned to love work for at least two reasons: First, labor helped Washington to develop his own moral agency. Second, he came to understand and love work because, properly ordered, it provides value to other people.

To the first point, labor taught Washington the "independence and self-reliance" that accompanies "the ability to do something which the world wants done."[14] It gave him the essential skills to develop his own moral life, including the virtues that are necessary for that development. Washington was learning to "subdue the earth," joining the co-creative work of God, and thereby refining his own moral skill.

As Pope St. John Paul II explains in *Laborem Exercens*, work expresses and expands the dignity of the human person. Work is good, at least in part, "because through work man *not only transforms nature*, adapting it to his own needs, but he also *achieves fulfillment* as a human being."[15] By his co-creative activity with God, the human person develops his own nature as made in the very image of God as Creator. John Paul calls this the "virtue of industriousness."[16] This is not to ignore the ways in which work, especially forced work or work under immoral circumstances, is detrimental to the human person. In these cases, work does not contribute to the development of the human person, but rather detracts from it, lowering the dignity of man rather than elevating it.[17] This is why, John Paul insists, work must be understood within the full social teaching of the Church. This teaching prioritizes the subjective nature of work, which I discuss more fully below.

The development of the moral virtues is closely related to the second reason that Booker T. Washington learned to love labor: because it provides value to others. Through work, we are able to serve our neighbors. Through his labor as a janitor at Hampton, Washington explains, "I got my first taste of what it meant to live a life of unselfishness."[18] It was where he learned that "the happiest individuals are those who do the most to make others useful and happy."[19] Work not only provided sustenance, it also provided the moral foundation for his life of tireless service, which benefited the broader community. "Wherever one of our brickmakers has gone in the South," he writes about his time at Tuskegee, the graduate "has something to contribute to the well-being of the community." He has provided a good and service that made the others, "to a certain extent, dependent upon him."[20]

Washington accounts for work as an exercise in both solidarity and subsidiarity. The students at Tuskegee came together as one body to build the very institution that provided them the education and skills to negotiate the difficult life they faced in the wake of hundreds of years of slavery. Not all the students stayed, he tells us, because they could not embrace the difficult physical labor of making and laying bricks. But those who did stay developed the virtues attendant to an understanding of the solidarity of all humankind. They were joined in a common endeavor, but one that contributed to the well-being of each of them as developing moral agents. Solidarity expresses both the reality of our shared dignity as creatures made in the image and likeness of God, as well as the mandate to structure our lives consistent with that likeness. Work is an expression of both these examples of solidarity.

Washington's experience of work also reflects the Catholic doctrine of subsidiarity. As I suggested in chapter 3, we should think of subsidiarity primarily in terms of the help ("subsidy") that institutions provide to the moral development of the human agent. Not everyone is capable of making or laying bricks, planting crops, or raising livestock. By understanding that these things help others who are not able to do them for themselves, we see the nature of work serving this social good. Sometimes subsidiary functions emerge from the normal interactions between workers and the people they serve. At other times, it might be necessary to form more formal structures, such as guilds, labor unions, or trade associations. The measure of the need for such institutions is the assistance they give to others (including their own members), consistent with the development of the moral agent. While Washington was not Catholic, or formed by Catholic moral doctrine, he expressed what we might call the organic reality of these moral principles. They are not merely "Catholic"; they exist anywhere people have a true understanding of the nature and purpose of work.

The End of Work Is Not to Work

Booker T. Washington's real-life explanation of his experience of the social nature and utility of work is instructive as far as it goes. But his account of the goodness of work is not complete. In fact, he fails to account for the most important end or purpose of work. Put simply, the highest purpose of work is not to work. We see this both in the structure and the text of the first creation account in Genesis. "On the seventh day God completed the work he had been doing; he rested on the seventh day from all the work he had undertaken" (Gn 2:2). Of course, we understand that God does not need rest. God's being is God's act. He is inexhaustible in his presence and action. God "rests" not because he needs a break from the exertion of his work, but to demonstrate that work, while natural and good, points beyond itself to something higher. "God blessed the seventh day and made it holy, because on it he rested from all the work he had done in creation" (Gn 2:3). God later instructed Israel through Moses, "Remember the sabbath day — keep it holy" (Ex 20:8).

The purpose of resting from work is not simply to take a break from the toil and stress of labor so that we can do more work. While leisure may have the incidental effect of allowing us to return to work refreshed and reinvigorated, that is not the purpose of rest. As Catholic philosopher Josef Pieper notes in his landmark book *Leisure: The Basis of Culture*, "Leisure does not exist for the sake of work — however much strength it may give a man to work; the point of leisure is not to be a restorative, a pick-me-up, whether mental or physical; and though it gives new strength, mentally and physically, and spiritually too, that is not the point."[21] Rather, work points beyond itself to rest as a higher good. Important as work is, it is not an end in itself. Its purpose is to create the conditions that allow us not to work, but to take a substantive break from work to pursue higher things.

Of course, the immediate purpose of the Sabbath is to rest from work so we can worship God. To give God the worship he is due, we must be free from the constraint, rigor, and distraction of working. But the Sabbath rest is actually broader than worship. As I discussed in chapter 3, the dignity of the human person implies a sense of transcendence. This entails the quest for contemplation. Worship of God is the highest form of that contemplation, but it is not the only form. The enjoyment of art, music, family, sport, cinema, reading, civic and social engagement, travel, and a host of other goods is also an aspect of the human capacity for transcendent contemplation and the need to fulfill it. We must have the time and means to pause from work so that we may seek those nonmaterial goods which are unique to the human creature. Work serves that purpose.

In other words, work is ordered toward leisure. "Leisure, like contemplation, is of a higher order" than work, explains Pieper. This is the "order" that I discussed in chapter 2, rooted in the very story of creation. It is meant in the sense of being "ordered toward" something by nature or supernature. Pieper continues: "Order, in this sense, cannot be overturned or reversed. ... No one who looks to leisure simply to restore his working powers will ever discover the fruit of leisure."[22] The purpose of leisure is to pursue the higher goods, rooted in the transcendent nature of human dignity, that contribute to human flourishing. These higher goods are unique to the human person, made in the image and likeness of God. Leisure is the time and capacity to cultivate the human soul in all its transcendent goodness. The attainment of authentic leisure "is the power to overstep the boundaries of the workaday world and reach out to superhuman, life-giving existential forces that refresh and renew us."[23]

Leisure is for the fulfillment and flourishing of the human person; work is for creating the time and means for leisure. Therefore, the higher purpose of work is not the product made or the service provided, but the person who provides it. This introduces the important distinction between the "subjective" and "objective" dimensions of work, which in turn leads to a discussion of specific public policy options and considerations. These reflections are related to such things as workplace conditions, the relationship between employers and employees, the function of labor unions and similar associations, and the role of laws and regulations in the employment context. As with our discussion of the family in chapter 4, Catholic social doctrine suggests options that do not fall upon a continuum of "conservative" or "liberal" political opinions. Rather, built upon the four pillars of dignity, solidarity, subsidiarity, and the common good, the Catholic understanding of work transcends these partisan labels.

The Objective and Subjective Dimensions of Work

The objective dimension of work consists in the product made or the service provided. As the term implies, the *object* is the thing produced by the labor of the worker, and it exists outside the worker. The things that constitute the objective dimension are always changing as technological, social, regulatory, and legal conditions change over time. Products or services may become obsolete as they are replaced by newer, better methods or devices. For our consideration, the objective dimension of work is less important than the subjective dimension.

The subjective aspect of work considers both the contribution of the worker and the effect of the work on his moral development. But this does not mean that the objective dimension is not important at all. Some products or services can never be ordered toward true human good. Prostitution, pornography, surrogacy, and drug trafficking, for example, are all examples of the objective dimension of work, technically speaking, but none of them are consistent with the dignity of the human person or other aspects of Catholic moral theology. They are harmful to both their producers and consumers, and thus have no proper place in a just economy.

That said, however, our primary consideration is with the subjective dimension of work because, regardless of the product made or the service provided, this dimension of work is constant across time and contingencies. Assuming that the objective dimension of work does not violate some principle of Catholic morality, the subjective dimension still requires our consideration. This is because the subjective dimension contributes to (or detracts from) the growth and development of the person doing the work. Even work that produces a socially good product or service might be detrimental to the flourishing of the human person if it is not properly contextualized in a theology of work that respects the human subject involved in its creation. The subjective dimension of work calls into consideration such concerns as working conditions, wages, benefits, hours, the relationship of the worker to his work, and other aspects of work that affect the soul of the worker.

As a guiding principle, all work must prioritize the dignity of the worker as a moral agent. The worker must never be treated as a mere instrument, like any commodity or machine. This is what Pope St. John Paul II calls the "priority of labor over capital."[24] The worker is the primary cause of the production, while capital (broadly understood as every element other than the worker) is the mere instrument. Failure to prioritize the worker dehumanizes labor, stripping work of its dignity and its contribution to the well-being of the worker. This violates the bedrock Catholic moral principle that people may never be used as a mere means to some end.

The worker cannot be treated as a mere commodity, whose services are sold and purchased as though the person who provided them were nothing more than raw material, parts, or machinery. As *Gaudium et Spes* puts it, "Human labor ... is superior to the other elements of economic life, for the latter have only the nature of tools."[25] Granted, the various stages of economic development since the nineteenth century have made labor look more and more like a commodity. Many employers consider workers nothing other than vendors of their time or skill. But the subjective dimension of work entails psychological, moral, and social investment by the worker. He is not merely selling a skill, but entering into a cooperative, creative endeavor.

Employers can recognize and honor the subjective dimension by humanizing the work and work environment, and giving the employee a stake in the creative process. This can be accomplished, for example, through employee recognition programs, employer/employee committees or counsels, or other cooperative endeavors between the worker and the employer.

Failure to honor the subjective dimension of work results in alienation of the worker, both from the product or service he provides (or contributes to) and from his employer. This alienation goes to the heart of the Marxist critique of capitalism. While the solutions proposed by Marx and his heirs are not compatible with Catholic theology, we cannot ignore the critique where it is well-founded. The way toward a solution is to recognize labor not as a commodity to be purchased by the employer, but as an investment by the employee in the endeavor. Rather than viewing employer and employee as antagonists in a commercial transaction, a truly Catholic view would envision them as cooperating in a common enterprise. Instead of bidding for the most work for the least money, the employer should engage the human person, inviting him to share a particular vision of the product to be manufactured and sold, or the service to be provided. This is a form of solidarity. In the ideal case it is not simply the solidarity of the employees against the employer, but rather all concerned in the enterprise in solidarity with one another.

When the employer and employee are not able to reach this solidarity, it may be necessary for the employees to pool their resources in solidarity with one another in the form of a labor union. Labor unions are noble and honorable institutions that have served to protect the dignity of workers against employers who have exploited their workers and alienated them from the work. The Church has highly valued the place of labor unions guarding the well-being of workers, especially where technology and industry seem to outpace moral reflection and action. Pope Leo XIII refers to labor unions as "the most important" of cooperative societies of workers.[26] Where properly constituted and managed, labor unions give workers legitimate leverage to negotiate for better working conditions, higher wages, or a place at the decision-making table. They may also pool employee funds to provide safeguards against layoffs or safety nets in the event of economic downturns or workplace calamities or accidents.

Of course, as illustrated in Elia Kazan's masterful film *On the Waterfront*, unions are as susceptible to mismanagement and corruption as any other human institution.[27] Additionally, unions fail their members when they advocate for political candidates or social policies that are not directly in service of their mission to serve all their constituent members. The need to guard and reform unions when this occurs is no different from the need with any other human institution that strays from or fails in its proper mission.

Moreover, important as unions are — and as wholly legitimate as they are when needed — the presence of strong unions might be seen as a failure of employee and employer to reach a mutually agreeable consensus on the enterprise. I want to be careful and clear in this discussion so that I am not misunderstood. Labor unions are valued and honored institutions, enjoying the full favor and support of the Church through her social doctrine. Unions are a legitimate expression of the solidarity of workers as they join in a united enterprise to protect themselves against both hostile employers and economic turbulence. And they have had a positive social impact on workers and their families for generations. Many of the perquisites and benefits that we take for granted in the workplace — such as health insurance, paid vacations, safety regulations, and overtime pay — exist because of the salutary presence of unions in American economic life. As Pope St. John Paul II put it, the work of labor unions "should be seen as a normal endeavor 'for' the just good, ... *not* a *struggle 'against' others*." The union "remains a constructive factor of *social order* and *solidarity*."[28]

Having said that, however, the good of labor unions for workers might be likened to the good of medicine for the body. Medicine is a good thing. It should be seen as part of the "normal endeavor" to treat illness. Where a person has chronic health issues, the ongoing use of medicine contributes both to his good and the good of society more generally. But medicine is only required when the body is not functioning as it should. The better situation is a healthy body, in which the parts are all working properly and in harmony with one another, where no medicine is needed. We do not disparage medicine when it is needed, but we recognize that it is "better" when it is not needed. Labor unions can be seen in a similar way. Where the workplace is one of harmony and cooperation, in which employers and employees engage in a common enterprise, rowing in the same direction and in the same rhythm, the need for labor unions is lessened if not, in some cases, eliminated. The better path is for labor and capital to work in harmony with one another, working toward common goals, and always with the moral development of the worker in mind.

Solidarity should not be confined to workers, but should include elements of the entire business enterprise: workers, managers, and owners alike. It might even be institutionalized by a formal structure that looks something like a union, but is founded upon mutual cooperation and respect rather than antagonism. Such a structure would include representatives from all facets of the enterprise. As Pope Leo XIII said all the way back in 1891, "It is gratifying to know that there are actually in existence ... associations of this nature, consisting ... of workmen and employers together."[29]

These kinds of structures meet the needs of both employer and employee outside the rigid regulations of formal unions, and they are a better indication of the health of the business. Thus they contribute to the social principle of subsidiarity. Laborers, managers, and owners help one another at the most local and immediate place available, without having to enlist regulatory or legal structures to keep everyone in line. Smart business managers, even those with no training in Catholic social teaching, see the value in addressing the needs of their employers, rather than allowing problems to fester until the intrusive hand of government is required. Of course, such cooperation is built upon the foundation of the dignity of the worker, whose presence in the enterprise is a good in itself, not merely the means to a profit. And the good that is achieved in such a state of affairs benefits everyone involved in the business, which is to say that it contributes to the common good.

What Is a "Just" Wage?

Probably the most challenging aspect of a theology of work is the issue of fair compensation to the worker, consistent with the dignity of work, the subjective moral agency of the worker, and the common good. The *Catechism* declares, "A *just wage* is a legitimate fruit of work. To refuse or withhold it can be a grave injustice" (2434). But what is a just wage, and how is it measured? *Gaudium et Spes* offers a very general definition, but it is so highly qualified that it leaves many questions unanswered: "Remuneration for labor is to be such that man may be furnished the means to cultivate worthily his own material, social, cultural, and spiritual life and that of his dependents, in view of the function and productiveness of each one, the conditions of the factory or workshop, and the common good."[30] This suggests that just compensation for work may take a variety of forms, dependent upon a host of variable factors. Moreover, it leaves room for the possibility (if not probability) that a wage might be just even if, in some cases, it is not what we might call a "family" or "living" wage.

Political philosopher J. Brian Benestad, who taught Catholic Social Doctrine for many years at the University of Scranton before moving to his current position at Assumption College in Worcester, Massachusetts, is among the preeminent scholars in the field. In his book *Church, State, and Society*, Benestad suggests six principles of a just wage, which are helpful in thinking through this difficult issue.[31] But the principles also point out the tension inherent in this discussion. According to Benestad, a just wage:

1. Must be sufficient to ensure what's necessary and fitting for the worker
2. Must be sufficient to procure what is necessary and fitting for the support of a family
3. Must be proportionate to the productivity of the work of each company
4. Must be in harmony with the requirements of the common good
5. Must allow the worker the possibility of acquiring property

6. Must allow the worker to satisfy the more noble human aspirations (e.g., participating in public life and having sufficient resources to educate children according to their capacities)[32]

Benestad suggests that numbers "one, two, five, and six should be the goals of every employer and economic system."[33] If he means that failure of every job to meet all four of these principles would be unjust, I do not agree. For example, the first principle might be met, but fall short of the second, without resulting in an injustice. A "necessary and fitting" wage for a teenager in his first job at the corner coffee shop can be a just wage even though it would not support a family. Even if the job pays an hourly *wage* that might support a family if multiplied by a forty-hour week, the analysis does not end there. The shop might only operate for breakfast or lunch hours, for example, making it impossible for such an annual salary to be reached without doubling or tripling the hourly wage, which would not be sustainable for the business. Surely, by itself, this does not make the wage "unjust." In fact, the third principle set forth above suggests that such a wage may be just. The wage in my hypothetical coffee shop is "proportionate to the productivity of the work" of the company, but falls well short of a wage that would support a family.

This suggests that a just wage is not necessarily equivalent to a family wage or a living wage. It also suggests that a minimum wage might pass muster as a just wage without being enough to sustain a family. But the principles Benestad lists are still helpful, because taken together they tell us that we do not measure the justice of a wage simply by the contractual agreement between the employer and the employee.

Sometimes an economy may be so compromised by unjust monopoly control, artificial inflationary pressures, unfair export barriers, a glut of labor, or other factors that the conditions themselves render a just contract impossible. We cannot measure the justice of remuneration simply on the terms of an employment contract. As the *Catechism* puts it, "Agreement between the parties is not sufficient to justify morally the amount to be received in wages" (2434). Rather, we must also look at the external conditions that might render that agreement itself unjust, because they make it impossible for the worker to bargain fairly.

Of course, this is where the government might have to step in under the principle of subsidiarity. Laws and regulations that help to eliminate unfair employer advantages are legitimate to the extent that such advantages cannot be otherwise remedied. Similarly, publicly funded technical, vocational, or other kinds of training may help to prepare workers for jobs for which they would otherwise be unqualified. Private/public partnerships, such as government-subsidized apprentice or internship programs, might also be implemented. Even with these measures, no economy can sustain a labor market in which every job in every industry has to be able to supply a family wage. Thus I suggest three proposals for an alternative way of thinking about a living or family wage that preserves the justice of wages that pay less.

The first proposal is that companies that *can* pay a living wage *must* pay that wage, even if the labor market might allow the employer to pay less. Of course, this will have an impact on the company's profitability. But we do not measure the justice of the employer/employee relationship solely on the bottom-line profit. A company operating under principles of Catholic social doctrine will pay a wage proportionate to its income and other costs, with a view toward the dignity of the worker and the common good. If a company follows this proposal, it also meets the doctrine of subsidiarity, because it resolves the issue in the most immediate manner.

Second, government policy should have as its goal an economic environment in which a living wage is available to everyone who seeks it. Such a policy would recognize that there will always be workers who do not seek a living wage and employers that cannot provide one. But the government will work to sustain the legal and regulatory structures that help sustain a market in which the number of jobs that can sustain family wages is equal to workers who need them. Not every wage would be a living wage, but a living wage would be available to all who need it. This might include offering income subsidies or tax incentives for businesses and industries. (Remember: The idea that government has no role in regulating the labor market is informed by liberal political theory, not Catholic social doctrine.)

The third proposal is that families take a harder look at what is necessary for a living wage. Jobs will always be scarce, regardless of how well-regulated markets are, or how robust the economy is. If one family has two salaries, either of which is sufficient to sustain the family and provide the leisure toward which work must point, and one of those jobs could be filled by a family that has none, principles of Catholic social doctrine suggest that the two-income family might be called to reduce their income by giving up one of those jobs.

At this point I need to be very clear. I am not suggesting that two-income families are necessarily committing an injustice. Unless and until my second proposal is met, some (indeed, many) families will require two incomes even for minimum sustainability. These families should not be disparaged or condemned. Additionally, it may often be the case that the employees in two-income families provide specialized skills or services, such that the common good would be diminished by one of them leaving his or her job. In that case, other moral principles might apply, such as the demands of charity or hospitality. But where these or other special circumstances do not obtain, and where the second salary finances frivolities while another family suffers, solidarity and the common good might suggest "sharing" that second job. Is this a radical idea? From the standpoint of libertarianism, in which morality is only measured by the license of an individual to do as he pleases, I suppose that it is. But Catholic moral doctrine is not libertarian economic theory.

Work in the Broader Economy

This chapter has discussed various aspects of work without reference to the broader economic systems or conditions in which the employer and employee play their respective roles in a business enterprise. But no business or industry exists outside the philosophical, legal, regulatory, and social elements that constitute an economy. So our discussion now turns to the Church's teaching on the economy, including the place of businesses in all their constituent parts.

Chapter 6
Economic Life: Money, Markets, and Morality

The Church has consistently condemned collectivist economic systems that deny the moral propriety of private property. Pope Leo XIII wrote, "It is clear that the main tenet of socialism, community of goods, must be utterly rejected, since it only injures those whom it would seem meant to benefit."[1] Invoking Leo, in 1931, Pope Pius XI declared, "Socialism ... cannot be reconciled with the teachings of the Catholic Church because its concept of society itself is utterly foreign to Christian truth."[2] Thus, "no one can be at the same time a good Catholic and a true socialist."[3]

Still, Pius, like his predecessor and successors, acknowledged the legitimacy of some socialist aspirations and goals — goals that capitalism also cannot meet. If capitalism results in the concentration of power in a few, and if it reduces all social life to an economic equation, it is no less pernicious than socialism.[4] While some goals of socialism are laudable, and some aspects of capitalism are commendable, Catholic social doctrine in its first hundred years consistently condemned socialism and never endorsed capitalism. As Pope St. John Paul II put it, "The Church's social doctrine adopts a critical attitude towards both liberal capitalism and Marxist collectivism."[5]

In this historical framework, on May 1, 1991, John Paul II promulgated *Centesimus Annus* commemorating the one hundredth anniversary of *Rerum Novarum*. Written during the upheaval caused by the collapse of the Soviet Union and its satellite vassal states in eastern Europe, *Centesimus Annus* made a clear but guarded statement about the kind of economic system that is most consistent with the nature of the human person as a creative moral agent, made in the image and likeness of God.

After the collapse of communism, Pope John Paul asked, "Can it perhaps be said that … capitalism is the victorious social system, and that capitalism should be the goal of the countries now making efforts to rebuild their economy and society?"[6] The answer is complex, but it begins with a straightforward acknowledgment, followed by a careful qualification. He continued:

> If by "capitalism" is meant an economic system which recognizes the fundamental and positive role of business, the market, private property and the resulting responsibility for the means of production, as well as free human creativity in the economic sector, then the answer is certainly in the affirmative, even though it would perhaps be more appropriate to speak of a "business economy," "market economy" or simply "free economy."[7]

This is not, however, an endorsement of an unfettered, unregulated, *laissez-faire* economy that fails to consider the dignity of the human person:

> If by "capitalism" is meant a system in which freedom in the economic sector is not circumscribed within a strong juridical framework which places it at the service of human freedom in its totality, and which sees it as a particular aspect of that freedom, the core of which is ethical and religious, then the reply is certainly negative.[8]

The measure of a just economic system is the dignity of the human person. The name of the system is less important than the extent to which it is consistent with human flourishing and the good of the human person.

Thus "the Church has no models to present," because different historical situations might present different frameworks for a just economic system. Instead, "the Church offers her social teaching as an indispensable and ideal orientation, a teaching which ... recognizes the positive value of the market and of enterprise, but which at the same time points out that these need to be oriented towards the common good."[9] Pope John Paul II's carefully qualified acknowledgment of the legitimacy of the "business economy" on the one hand, and his refusal to endorse any specific model on the other, is instructive for the way that we think about the good of a free economy. He was even reluctant to use the word *capitalism* because both proponents and opponents can latch onto the term either to champion or condemn *Centesimus Annus*, without taking into consideration the full rationale of his endorsement of the market economy.

For that reason, John Paul does not endorse an economic *system*. Rather, he acknowledges the good of economic structures that value the creative dynamism of the human spirit. His reasoning does not begin with sources of capital, but rather with the source of productive energy, which is the human moral agent, created in the image and likeness of God. Imagination, innovation, and experimental risk-taking are all aspects of this image. It does not matter what you call a particular economic arrangement. Rather, what matters is how that arrangement values, supports, and benefits from the creative spirit of the human person. Laws and administrative regulations then create and sustain the infrastructure that supports and advances this creativity.

In the same way, when aspects of "capitalism" inhibit the creative agency of the human person, or when they tend to exploit some for the gain of others, a just arrangement will correct those elements. For example, a person's natural creative ability might need training and education to reach its full capacity. Economic structures that do not develop such facilities may have to be supplemented by public programs that fill the gaps. This might be done through publicly funded training programs or even wealth transfers that allow access to such resources. Some people reflexively label such programs as "socialism," and thus condemn them. But these kinds of measures are not only consistent with a market economy, they also help to support and advance it. Better, they help to support and advance the human person, toward which the market economy should be ordered. This is because the measure of the good of any economic arrangement is the flourishing of the human person, who is at the center of all economic considerations. The "dignity and complete vocation of the human person and the welfare of society as a whole are to be respected and promoted," explains *Gaudium et Spes*. "For man is the source, the center, and the purpose of all economic and social life."[10]

The good of a market economy is found in its consistency with the co-creative nature of the human person, working in free cooperation with others. Even before the exchange of goods and services in the marketplace, a free economy, properly channeled and regulated, both reflects and facilitates the solidarity of humankind. This cooperation creates the wealth that contributes to the good of all. "A person who produces something other than for his own use generally does so in order that others may use it after they have paid a just price, mutually agreed upon through free bargaining,"[11] explains John Paul. This highlights "the *role* of disciplined and creative *human work* and, as an essential part of that work, *initiative and entrepreneurial ability*."[12] Important moral virtues are required for this process, including "diligence, industriousness, prudence in undertaking reasonable risks, reliability and fidelity in interpersonal relationships, as well as courage in carrying out decisions."[13]

But this confirmation of market elements as part of a just economic system is not an endorsement of unfettered and unregulated libertarian economics. The primary focus is never on the product created, the service provided, or the well-being of the business. Nor should deference be given to the source of capital over the good of the worker. These are all good and necessary elements of a just economy. But they are all necessary means toward the proper end of the good of the human person. The elevation of the person, not profitability, is the proper object even of a free economy.

A business "cannot be considered only as a 'society of capital goods,'" continues Pope John Paul; "it is also a 'society of persons' in which people participate in different ways." A just economy is one that leads to the "liberation and promotion of the whole person."[14] This is in contrast to economic structures that place profit over persons, or that exploit workers for the sake of the bottom line. When "man is seen more as a producer or consumer of goods than as a subject who produces and consumes in order to live, then economic freedom loses its necessary relationship to the human person and ends up by alienating and oppressing him."[15]

This is an important caution to some proponents of capitalism, who would reduce the human person to nothing more than a producer, customer, or consumer, and human relationships to nothing other than commercial transactions. When we emphasize a system over persons, we tend to lose sight of the person to whose good any system must be ordered. Capitalism has an inherent tendency to reduce human persons to economic units, measuring their worth not by their inherent dignity but rather by their contribution to the market, either as producers or consumers of goods. Thus producing and consuming become ends, to which the human person is no more than a means. "This is the so-called civilization of 'consumption' or 'consumerism,'" complains Pope St. John Paul II.[16] Such a reduction of the human person to an economic unit is no less dehumanizing than socialist systems that have the same essential effect. We are not the sum of our productive ability or material desires. Rather, those human qualities are means of achieving the higher goods that contribute to the full flourishing of the human person.

Regulation of Market Economies

The better way for markets to be regulated is through the free cooperation between and among owners, workers, and customers. A network of collaboration serves the goal of subsidiarity, as mutual benefit emerges from this kind of collaboration. But when cooperation fails, when profit becomes an end in itself, or where workers are exploited for the good of the bottom line, it may become necessary for larger subsidiary spheres to step in to regulate markets. This might involve, for example, regulations on working hours and workplace conditions, paid family leave, minimum wage requirements or incentives, and guaranteed minimum incomes.

Again, this presents the central theme of this book. The

good of such governmental or bureaucratic intervention in the economy is not measured by its consistency with one political party or another, but rather by its contribution to the good of the human person. An economic system must be at the service of the human person. Where this is compromised, governmental intervention is not merely a necessary, but a *just* measure. "Economic activity, especially the activity of a market economy, cannot be conducted in an institutional, juridical or political vacuum," explains Pope John Paul II.[17] Governments have "a duty to sustain business activities by creating conditions which will ensure job opportunities, by stimulating those activities where they are lacking or by supporting them in moments of crisis."[18]

Some goods and services, regardless of how much wealth they generate, can never serve the common good or the dignity of the human person. Pornography, illicit drugs, prostitution, elective abortion, and surrogate "parenting" are but a few examples of industries that might flourish in a free economy, but which serve only to degrade human dignity and violate the common good. Laws and regulations that prohibit or forbid such activities, even if those measures are not consistent with some conceptions of a "free" economy, are just measures to preserve the dignity of all persons and the common good.

On the other hand, some of the highest human goods cannot be supplied by market economics or any other economic system. Again, the purpose of the economy is to provide the means to pursue those higher goods, but a healthy economy recognizes that the market is not an end itself. Human flourishing requires time and liberty to pursue such intermediary institutions as social clubs, fraternal organizations, charitable endeavors, and the enjoyment of leisurely pursuits in the arts, sport, and worship. When social cooperation in the economy provides for this pursuit, subsidiarity requires that governments step back. When the unregulated market itself does not contribute to the space and time for such goods — when it needs help to provide them — governmental intervention is consistent with the doctrine of subsidiarity. As noted in chapter 3, subsidiarity is measured by the appropriate level of assistance for human flourishing, not merely by the proximity or size of the helping institution. Therefore, government "has a duty to sustain business activities by creating conditions which will ensure job opportunities, by stimulating those activities where they are lacking or by supporting them in moments of crisis."[19] This should be government *assistance*, not *substitution*. Interventions should be close to the issue and as brief as possible, so that the proximate institutions are not subsumed under the remote. Interventions in the market may be necessary, but they should "avoid enlarging excessively the sphere of State intervention to the detriment of both economic and civil freedom."[20] This is the delicate balance between subsidiarity and solidarity. Solidarity suggests that helping intervention may sometimes be required. Subsidiarity suggests that this intervention should be carefully measured and guarded, so that human agency is not lost in a sea of bureaucracy and regulation.

The Universal Destination of Goods and Preferential Option for the Poor

There are two essential implications of the doctrine of the common good that we must consider when discussing economic life. These two things are what the Church calls the "universal destination of goods" and the "preferential option for the poor," two essential implications of the doctrine of the common good. The universal destination of goods is rooted in the reality that God created all things, and that all things are for the good of the whole of humanity. We are not the originators of anything that exists; neither are we absolute owners of anything, allowing us to do with it as we will, without concern for the effect on the common good. Because God creates all things, all things are created for the use and good of all. What we call private ownership is really stewardship. Ownership is a necessary component of the efficient use and distribution of human goods. But it is not absolute; nor is it immune from regulation when it is used to exploit others.

The preferential option for the poor is what we might call a "filter" for the way we consider any economic policy. Regardless of the context in which the policy is being proposed, we must always be mindful of its effect on the poor. Does the policy contribute to the development of all people? Or does it favor the "haves" over the "have nots"? We must prefer policies that contribute to the good of all, and shape economic policy accordingly.

To be sure, the Church recognizes the propriety of private property, which was assumed and protected as early as the Ten Commandments. The commands not to steal or covet necessarily imply the legitimacy of ownership. Jesus, in his parables and associations, acknowledges the good of private, personal property. But private ownership is qualified by the reminder that we are *stewards* of the things that God has created. We are not *lords* over any part of God's creation that we might possess. To the extent that human creativity contributes to the development of wealth, it is only because we have collaborated with what we have been given. But "the possession of material goods is not an absolute right," explains Pope St. John Paul II.[21] Rather, private property "is under a 'social mortgage,' which means that it has an intrinsically social function."[22] Personal possession of wealth is "*based upon and justified* precisely by the principle of the universal destination of goods."[23]

This might seem like a contradiction. If goods are universally destined for the good of all, how can it be good for some people to "own" property? The universal destination of goods, in the context of the co-creative capacity of the human person, implies the *development* of goods and the *creation* of wealth. These can only happen efficiently in the context of persons having title to property that they can improve, develop, or put at risk. As the ignominious histories of collectivist economies have unanimously demonstrated, development of goods and creation of wealth do not occur when private property is not protected and return on risk is not guarded.

Still, the development of goods and creation of wealth should be ordered toward the dignity of all persons and the achievement of the common good. This means that in making economic decisions, whether on the level of the person, family, community, or nation, we must have a preferential option for the poor. Any discussion of the development of economic life, the regulation of markets and exchanges, the levying of taxes and fees, and the distribution of wealth must be in the context of their effects on the poor. Do our policies contribute to the development of the poor, or to their further impoverishment?

This does not mean that redistribution should be the first impulse. Creative regulatory infrastructures that allow and protect access to labor markets, incentivize private and institutional charity, and otherwise create opportunities for the poor to be lifted from poverty should always be our social priority. Subsidiary institutions and regulations should assist the poor in developing their own creative capacities and skills. But neither does this preclude the role of redistribution of wealth, if properly conceived and executed. Tax rates for the wealthy and credits for the poor can also be legitimate ways of serving the principle of the preferential option for the poor. Balancing this with policies that protect and advance creativity is not a simple task. But the challenge of doing it right does not absolve us from failing to do it at all.

The Use of Wealth and Cooperation with Evil

The creation and distribution of wealth are not the only moral challenges in a free economy. The use to which we put our wealth is also an important consideration, especially if we are committed to the broad spaces that allow and even encourage expressive creativity and experimental entrepreneurship. How we spend and invest our money is as important a moral consideration as how we earn it. In the same way as there are some means of earning money that can never be consistent with Catholic moral life, so the purchase of some goods and services can never be ordered toward the good. The moral good of economic life cannot be reduced to one's absolute liberty to earn, spend, or invest as he wills. This is the error of unfettered or *laissez-faire* capitalism, sometimes called "libertarianism" in the American context.

Instead, we must consider how our investment and spending involve us in cooperation with evil. Such cooperation should, of course, be avoided where possible and mitigated when not. This presents yet another significant challenge, yielding no easy answer. The complexity of the national and international economy makes it impossible completely to avoid purchasing or investing that does not, even if very remotely, contribute to some aspect of some businesses to which we might have a moral objection. But we can address this problem in two stages, even if we can find no solution that gives us complete comfort. The first stage is to consider general Catholic teaching about cooperation with evil. The second is to examine specific industries or companies that should either be avoided or supported, and channel our purchasing and investing power accordingly.

The Church does not teach that all cooperation with evil is sinful. If it did, at least as applied to economic life, it would be virtually impossible to use money without sinning. But while we cannot avoid cooperation with evil, we can distinguish between kinds of cooperation, identifying what is tolerable and what is not.

The first distinction is whether the cooperation is "formal" or "material." Formal cooperation with evil is always illicit. It means that one deliberately engages with the evil act, intending the evil outcome itself. One agrees with the evil end of the action and assists another in obtaining that end. In the economic context, contributing to Planned Parenthood, for example, is formal cooperation with evil. Planned Parenthood's purpose is to distribute contraception and provide abortions. Thus to give money to such an organization is an expression of agreement with, and facilitation of, evil.

Material cooperation *may* be licit if other elements of the analysis are met. This cooperation with evil occurs when a person assists another in some endeavor that produces an evil action or outcome, but the person does not intend that outcome himself. His action in assisting the person or business is voluntary, but he does not intend the evil that is caused by the person or business. Material cooperation may be licit or illicit, depending on its relative causal proximity to the evil. If the material cooperation is immediate or proximate, it is always illicit. If the cooperation is mediate, it may be licit, even though other considerations may still counsel against it.

Immediate material cooperation occurs when a person does not agree with the outcome (as in formal cooperation), but participates in the execution of the outcome, nonetheless. An example of this problem often arises in the context of pharmaceuticals. Does the pharmacist who dispenses contraception prescriptions that he *knows* will be used for contraception (rather than some other therapeutic purpose) immediately cooperate with evil? This is a hard question, going right to the heart of work and economic life. Similar questions arise for technical and nursing staff at hospitals that perform so-called gender affirmation surgery or dispense puberty blockers or cross-sex hormones. Even if one disagrees with such procedures, does one immediately, materially cooperate if one prepares the surgery room, helps to prep the physician, or tends to the wounds of the victim?

Mediate material cooperation, on the other hand, occurs when a person cooperates with another in a way that does not intend and is not related to some evil that the other person may commit. One neither promotes nor facilitates the evil outcome, even if one knows that it will occur or there is a high probability that it will occur. This kind of cooperation with evil is, for all intents and purposes, impossible to avoid in our economy. For example, many consumer products and services are provided by companies that may contribute to charitable organizations to which we have moral objections. In some cases, *every* company that provides some essential service does this. Internet service providers, grocery store chains, online bookstores and other merchants, manufacturers of personal electronic devices, cellular service providers, department stores, drug stores, automobile manufacturers, and restaurant chains comprise a small sample from a very long list of companies that provide necessary goods and services, but that contribute time or money to morally objectionable causes.

Even in cases where there are alternatives to these companies, we cannot get away from the problem entirely. So, for example, one might choose to patronize a certain chicken sandwich restaurant because it is known to support causes and values that are morally praiseworthy. But that is not the end of the analysis. That restaurant does not manufacture its ovens and friers, fabricate its cups, package its ketchup, bake its buns, or deliver its supplies. These goods are all sourced from other vendors, the majority of which likely support the same objectionable causes that contradict our moral positions. Whether we like to admit it or not, when we buy that sandwich, we are cooperating with evil, albeit in a mediate, material way.

The analysis is similar for our investment dollars. We might think we are investing virtuously by avoiding companies that manufacture or distribute goods that are harmful to the human person and the common good. But if we have a 401(k), 403(b), or other employer-based retirement account, we are usually investing in mutual funds or exchange-traded funds, with very limited options. It is virtually certain that those funds own stock in companies that we consciously avoid investing in directly.

My point in this discussion of cooperation with evil is twofold. First, we certainly do have a moral obligation to refrain from formal cooperation with evil. We cannot purchase products from, or invest in, companies that manufacture goods or provide services that are evil. This includes abortion providers and purveyors of pornography as well as less obvious companies, such as manufacturers of certain kinds of guns or companies that are known to exploit the poor and marginalized, but are outside the reach of U.S. regulations.

On the other hand, we cannot smugly declare that we do not cooperate with evil because we do not purchase from or invest in X coffee shop, Y fast-food establishment, or Z electronic device manufacturer. As explained above, that is not the full measure of cooperation with evil. In the modern economy, it is simply not possible to avoid cooperating with evil in mediate, material, and remote ways. In other words, the best we can do is to avoid companies whose purpose is to produce goods or services that are morally objectionable, and minimize our exposure to those whose profits or advocacy are used for objectionable activities. We should be diligent, but we cannot be self-righteous.

The Accumulation of Wealth

The universal destination of goods speaks to the problem of the massive accumulation of wealth in the hands of the relatively few. We cannot make blanket assertions either about the propriety of such accumulation or the means to address it. The issue requires nuance and deliberation, and it yields no easy solution. For example, we must consider how the accumulation occurred. In the United States, some of the richest people and families are founders of small businesses that have become massive international companies. The wealth of such people as Bill Gates, Elon Musk, and Michael Dell, for example, is contained in their relative shares of companies that they founded. They took risks that have inured to the benefit of all.

This presents very challenging policy considerations. On the one hand, exercising entrepreneurial creativity and assuming the risks involved must be rewarded. If not, the risks will not be taken. On the other hand, can we really say that it is just for some people to amass tens of billions of dollars, while others struggle even to provide basic amenities through no fault of their own? Of course, the ideal solution is for those with massive amounts of wealth to distribute it in a manner that takes into account the universal destination of goods. Tax policy and other economic regulatory measures can be used to incentivize voluntary charitable activity. Government exists in part precisely for this role. If tax policies or other incentives for personal initiative are not sufficient, then we must ask whether and to what extent direct government action to redistribute wealth is appropriate. Surcharges on luxury goods, high marginal tax rates for the super wealthy, legally mandated distributions of stock options to employees, or regulation of such awards to management or board members might be ways to address disparities while preserving the just reward of economic risk.

Whatever shape such a discussion takes, it is crucial that we Catholics conduct it within the framework of Catholic social doctrine, not partisan politics. Neither of the major political parties in the United States is interested in balancing these delicate tasks. Ours must be a voice of practical reason, articulated in a moral vocabulary of dignity, solidarity, subsidiarity, and the common good, with a good dose of prudent deliberation. Justice is not measured merely by allowing people to accumulate what they have "earned" without taking into account the broader principle of the universal destination of goods. But neither can we simply confiscate wealth in such a way that creative incentive is squelched. In all things, we must remember that the human person is at the center of our deliberation, exercising his or her moral agency, with an end toward human flourishing.

Finally, the accumulation or use of wealth, whether in very small or very great amounts, must never be used to exploit or oppress the poor. In the Old Testament prophetic tradition, wealth itself is not condemned. Nor are the wealthy criticized on account of their wealth. Rather, the prophets denounce the wealthy (or anyone else) who use their relative economic advantage to exploit the poor and further oppress the outcast. The prophet Amos condemns Israel, for example, "because they hand over the just for silver, / and the poor for a pair of sandals" (Am 2:6). He decries those who "trample upon the needy, / and destroy the poor of the land," by fixing their scales to cheat the poor (see 8:4, 5b). "Oppressing the poor for enrichment, / giving to the rich: both are sheer loss," declares Proverbs 22:16. Also, "Whoever mocks the poor reviles their Maker; / whoever rejoices in their misfortune will not go unpunished" (Prv 17:5). The principle of the universal destination of goods teaches us that all the world's wealth is to be used for the benefit of all. To use wealth to accomplish the opposite — to oppress and exploit — is the gravest evil use of wealth.

Tying It All Together

Thus far, we have considered the source of Catholic social doctrine and the four pillars upon which it is built, and we have applied that consideration to analyze the family, work, and the economy. To conclude this book, I will turn to a consideration of political life, including the broad scope of our social and civic obligations, challenging us to revive a distinctly Catholic political language.

Chapter 7
Political Life: Civic Friendship and Christian Discipleship

I will begin this chapter with a list of paired statements.

- Christian faith is intrinsically political. But it cannot be identified with any specific politics.
- Christian theology endorses no particular model of politics. But it stands in critical judgment over all models.
- The human person is an essentially political being. But politics is not the end of human striving.
- The Church and government have distinct social roles. But those roles are necessarily interrelated.

- Christians have a duty to obey the laws of their nation. But they do not justify those laws by the laws' own terms, and they may be obligated to disobey them.
- Christians may be loyal to their homeland. But that loyalty is subordinated to Christian discipleship.
- Christians have a mandate to participate in civic life. But that mandate may require abstaining from political activity.
- Christian faith is the leaven of political life. But Christian faith is always subversive of any regnant politics.

These and other disjuncts are at the center of any discussion of the relationship between Christian faith and political life. Their confusion (or conflation) in the minds of many Americans is what motivated me to write this book. The best way to think of these pairs of contrasts is to keep them in tension with one another. By "tension," I do not mean "conflict," "strain," or "anxiety." Rather, the truth that emerges from these (and other) pairs of contrasts is found and sustained in the very tension between them. The tension is a feature, not a bug. It is like the surface tension in water, sustaining a ship. The tension will support the ship if it is composed of suitable material, fashioned into the appropriate shape, maintained at the proper weight, and its ballast duly distributed. If any of these factors fail, the ship may founder or sink. Tension keeps the ship afloat, and it tests the integrity of the ship and its crew.

While metaphors eventually always fail, this is a helpful way of considering the tension of these contrasting sets of statements about political life. Holding to both of each contrasting pair sustains a proper understanding of the relationship of faith to politics, and of the Christian to political life. Maintaining both tests the integrity of our faith. Like building and maintaining a seaworthy ship, it is hard work. Our Lord has promised us that the Barque of Peter will never sink, but that does not absolve us of our responsibility to be diligent in maintaining her seaworthiness. Careful consideration of the inherent tension in political life is essential to that diligence.

Each part of the pairs of contrasts above must be maintained. When one or the other is forgotten, or when the two become confused, we may find ourselves subordinating faith to politics. When that happens in the American context, it logically follows that we begin to derive our moral principles from one or the other of the two major political parties in the United States — which, as we have seen, represent two versions of the same moral theory of liberalism. This moral theory contains elements that are contradictory to Catholic moral doctrine, especially as it is expressed through the four pillars of Catholic social doctrine.

Christian moral theology sits in judgment over all politics, not to establish a particular political model, but to ensure that any political model is consistent with the good of the human person. The diligent judgment of theology over politics also ensures that we do not collapse the former into the latter, making an idol of political life. Christian faith transcends, relativizes, and subordinates all political claims. If we elevate political commitments over the claims of faith, or if we confuse the two with one another, we condemn ourselves to idolatry no less than if we were to bow to a golden calf.

Render to Caesar

One of the more perplexing encounters with Jesus in the Gospels illustrates the tension between Christian faith and political life. More important, however, it demonstrates that this tension is not a defect in a Christian consideration of political life, but rather an essential part of that discernment. All three of the

Synoptic Gospels recount the incident in which a group of Jesus' detractors attempt to coax him into making a treasonous statement about paying the census tax. The scene occurs in the week between Jesus' triumphant entry into Jerusalem and his crucifixion. The atmosphere is already thick with the political expectation of Jesus' followers and the political unease of Roman authorities and other critics. Both his supporters and opponents anticipate high political drama — perhaps even revolutionary violence — and the air is dense with anticipation.

In the midst of this excitement, as recorded in the Matthew 22:16–22, the Pharisees send an emissary to Jesus, initiating the following dialogue:

> "Teacher, we know that you are a truthful man and that you teach the way of God in accordance with the truth. ... Tell us, then, what is your opinion: Is it lawful to pay the census tax to Caesar or not?" Knowing their malice, Jesus said, "Why are you testing me, you hypocrites? Show me the coin that pays the census tax." Then they handed him the Roman coin. He said to them, "Whose image is this and whose inscription?" They replied, "Caesar's." At that he said to them, "Then repay to Caesar what belongs to Caesar and to God what belongs to God." When they heard this they were amazed, and leaving him they went away.

The Pharisees want either to discredit Jesus before his followers or to entrap him into advocating treachery. Instead, they elicit a profound truth from him about the relationship of his followers to the Roman government (and government more generally). Jesus sets aside the Pharisees' nefarious purpose and provides an answer that contributes to our understanding of the necessary role of government and our qualified acknowledgment of its legitimacy. And by not resolving the question, Jesus shows us that the tension is a necessary aspect of this relationship.

If Jesus had simply answered that it is legitimate to pay the tax with the Roman coin, it would have signified unqualified obedience to the sovereign, as though religious commitment was irrelevant to the responsibility to obey the law or otherwise to adhere to the demands of the state. Or, worse, it might have signified that Caesar himself was divine. This would have crushed the expectation of Jesus' followers, of course, because they were looking for a revolutionary leader who would unequivocally repudiate the legitimacy of Roman rule.

On the other hand, if Jesus had answered that it is not lawful to pay the tax, he would have instigated police action against himself. Such a statement would have been grounds for a capital charge of treason and suborning sedition on the part of his followers, leading to his probable immediate arrest. It is noteworthy in this regard to recall the interaction between Pilate and Jesus' accusers on Holy Friday. Flatly contradicting Jesus' answer about the tax, his accusers lied to Pilate, "We found this man misleading our people; he opposes the payment of taxes to Caesar" (Lk 23:2). After an inquiry, however, Pilate discerned that the accusation was false. "You brought this man to me and accused him of inciting the people to revolt," he told the crowd. "I have conducted my investigation in your presence and have not found this man guilty of the charges you have brought against him" (v. 14). When the crowd, now disillusioned because Jesus was not the violent revolutionary they desired, persisted, Pilate said, "What evil has this man done? I found him guilty of no capital crime" (v. 22).

The Caesar's coin pericope is both a pivotal scene in the Holy Week narrative, and vitally informative to us. The truth about the relationship between faith and politics is found in the tension between the two unqualified answers that Jesus did *not* give. He did not repudiate the tax (or the coin used to pay it), thus acknowledging the legitimate role of government and obedience to it. The implication is that even bad government may have legitimate aspects. But, of course, Jesus did not leave it at that. After confirming the image and inscription of Caesar on the coin, he said, "Then repay to Caesar *what belongs to Caesar.*" In the same breath, however, he added, "and to God what belongs to God" (Mt 22:21, emphasis added).

The set of things that belong to government is legitimate but narrowly defined. Of the two groups Jesus mentions, one is the small group that bears the seal of government; the other is the group that bears the image and likeness of God — humankind. Give the first to Caesar, says Jesus. Give the other to God. As I discuss below, this does not mean that government's relatively small realm is unqualified or independent of God's sovereignty. But for the purpose of making the contrast, the Caesar's coin narrative is highly instructive. Government's realm is legitimate but highly circumscribed. God's is broad and deep.

Among others, Saint Augustine seized upon this contrast to explain the fuller meaning of the Caesar's coin passage. Augustine wrote (as quoted in a homily by Pope Benedict XVI), "If Caesar reclaims his own image impressed on the coin, will not God demand from man the divine image sculpted within him? ... As the tribute money is rendered to him [Caesar], so should the soul be rendered to God, illumined and stamped with the light of his countenance."[1] Pope Benedict goes on to explain that the Caesar's coin passage is about much more than mere political life. "The word of Jesus is rich in anthropological content and it cannot be reduced only to the political context," he explains. "The Church ... is not limited to reminding human beings of the right distinction between the sphere of Caesar's authority and that of God. ... The mission of the Church ... is essentially to speak of God, to remember his sovereignty, to remind all, especially Christians who have lost their own identity, of the right of God to what belongs to him, that is, our life."² This is the perfect transition to Saint Paul's further elucidation on the role of government, and the tension between political and religious life.

Obedience to Whom It Is Due

After the Caesar's coin narrative, the most prominent passage in the New Testament related to government is found in the Letter of Saint Paul to the Romans. The passage is worth quoting in full to get the entire context:

> Let every person be subordinate to the higher authorities, for *there is no authority except from God*, and those that exist have been established by God. Therefore, whoever resists authority opposes what *God has appointed*, and those who oppose it will bring judgment upon themselves. For rulers are not a cause of fear to good conduct, but to evil. Do you wish to have no fear of authority? Then do what is good and you will receive approval from it, *for it is a servant of God* for your good. But if you do evil, be afraid, for it does not bear the sword without purpose; it is the servant of God to inflict wrath on the evildoer. Therefore, it is necessary to be subject not only because of the wrath but also because of conscience. This is why you also pay taxes, for the *authorities are ministers of God*, devoting themselves to this very thing. Pay to all their dues, taxes to whom taxes are due, toll to whom toll is due, respect to whom respect is due, honor to whom honor is due. (Romans 13:1–7, emphases added)

Not surprisingly, Paul's admonition is perfectly consistent with Jesus' statement from the Gospels. Government has a legitimate function. Paul expands on the teaching, however, by explaining that government is "a servant of God" for our good, and that public authorities are "ministers of God." Except that God has established it, "there is no authority." This way of stating the matter enhances our understanding of political authority in two ways.

First, earthly government is legitimate *because* it is a participation in the sovereignty of God. We owe obedience to government because it is one aspect of God's rule on earth. The order that comes from a system of laws, regulations, and policy commitments is necessary to preserve the common good, with all its constitutive parts. This is why Saint Paul explains that obedience to civil authority should not be motivated by fear, but rather an expression of moral commitment. We are obedient to the laws "because of conscience," not because of the threat of sanction. Civic cooperation is an aspect of our moral lives. To the extent that government is a legitimate expression of God's will, our obedience to the laws is obedience to God.

But this brings us to the second important implication of Saint Paul's teaching. Because government authority is a minister of God, its authority is legitimate only when it is consistent with God's will. A minister speaks on behalf of his superior as a proxy or agent. Like any other kind of proxy, government is illegitimate when it attempts to impose rule or power that is not consistent with the entity in whose place it purports to speak. The lives and deaths of Saints Peter and Paul are ready examples of this. Both were imprisoned and killed because they refused to obey the Roman government when it forbade them from preaching the Gospel.

Nothing evil can come from God. Thus when government acts in an evil way — broadly understood as contrary to God's will — it is no longer a legitimate minister of God, and therefore no longer commands obedience. This is why the last sentence of the passage quoted above is so important: "Pay to all their *dues*, taxes to whom taxes are *due*, toll to whom toll is *due*, respect to whom respect is *due*, honor to whom honor is *due*." Authority is from God, and this authority is not absolute. Thus neither is our obligation to obey it. We are to pay to Caesar what is *due* to Caesar. Saint Paul instructs us to pay taxes, tolls, and even respect and honor to government when they are due.

Saint Paul is describing the Christian virtue of justice. "*Justice* is the moral virtue that consists in the constant and firm will to give their due to God and neighbor," explains the *Catechism*. It is the virtue that "disposes one to … establish in human relationships the harmony that promotes equity with regard to persons and to the common good" (1807). Thus one exercises the moral virtue of justice when one gives to government what government is due — when one obeys just laws. Of course, this necessarily implies that government must act in accordance with principles of justice — otherwise, things like taxes, tolls, obedience, honor, and respect are not due to that government. Our duties may vary according to any number of historical and social contingencies. Temporary emergencies or crises may change the things that are due to the government, but when those emergencies are resolved, the "things" due the government are no longer due. We saw such an example with the COVID-19 pandemic in 2020.

But what about instances in which governments do not act in accordance with principles of justice? What is "due" then? To put it another way, what is our duty toward laws that are deviations from the role of government as God's minister for good? Sts. Augustine and Thomas Aquinas provide similar answers to this question. In listing a few hypothetical examples of what would be unjust laws, Augustine concludes, "What shall we dare say: that these laws are unjust, or rather that they are not laws? For it seems to me that an unjust law is not a law."[3] Thomas explains that an unjust law "is no longer a law, but a perversion of law."⁴ When this is the case, the authority of the government to enforce the law is nullified and, thus, the duty of the citizen to obey it is abrogated. "Laws can be unjust ... by being contrary to the divine good, as are laws that induce men ... to do anything ... that is contrary to divine law," concludes St. Thomas. "It is not permissible to obey such laws in any way at all."⁵

Martin Luther King Jr. famously cites both Augustine and Thomas in his Letter from Birmingham Jail, justifying disobedience to racially discriminatory laws. "A just law is a man made code that squares with the moral law or the law of God," explains King.⁶ "An unjust law is a code that is out of harmony with the moral law. To put it in the terms of St. Thomas Aquinas: An unjust law is a human law that is not rooted in eternal law and natural law."⁷ While he does not use the term *dignity* in this section of the letter, King invokes the concept in describing an example of a just law: "Any law that uplifts human personality is just. Any law that degrades human personality is unjust."⁸ King understood, in other words, that the end of law is not the law itself, nor even the good of the state. Rather, the end of law is the dignity of the human person.

This brings us back to Romans 13. Immediately following the discussion of the authority of government as a minister of God, Saint Paul gets to the finer point of justice — about who owes what to whom:

> Owe nothing to anyone, except to love one another; for the one who loves another has fulfilled the law. The commandments, "You shall not commit adultery; you shall not kill; you shall not steal; you shall not covet," and whatever other commandment there may be, are summed up in this saying, [namely] "You shall love your neighbor as yourself." Love does no evil to the neigh-

bor; hence, love is the fulfillment of the law. (Romans 13:8–10)

While he quotes from the Ten Commandments, Paul is clearly associating them with civil or political law. In other words, we cannot disassociate personal morality from public law and policy. At the end of the day, both must be expressions of charity, the form of the virtues.

Human law is not properly concerned with merely restraining bad behavior. Nor is it the purpose of law merely to adjudicate among competing rights. This liberal conception of law (whether from the right or left in its American expression) is very different from the conception of law that emerges from the Bible as developed in the Catholic Tradition. Rather, properly understood, laws and the governments that promulgate them ought to be ordered toward the good of the human person, fostering the conditions according to which we may fulfill our duty to love one another, and thus do justice. "We do not need a State which regulates and controls everything," explains Pope Benedict XVI in *Deus Caritas Est*, "but a State which, in accordance with the principle of subsidiarity, generously acknowledges and supports initiatives arising from the different social forces and combines spontaneity with closeness to those in need."[9]

This is the central theme of the second part of Pope Benedict's contribution to Catholic social doctrine. "Politics is more than a mere mechanism for defining the rules of public life," he explains; "its origin and its goal are found in justice, which by its very nature has to do with ethics."[10] The pope is careful to observe the distinction between the Church and the state; but he is also diligent in explaining the necessary connection between the two. "The two spheres are distinct, yet always interrelated."[11]

The Church cannot and must not take upon herself

the political battle to bring about the most just society possible. She cannot and must not replace the State. Yet at the same time she cannot and must not remain on the sidelines in the fight for justice. She has to play her part through rational argument and she has to reawaken the spiritual energy without which justice, which always demands sacrifice, cannot prevail and prosper. A just society must be the achievement of politics, not of the Church. Yet the promotion of justice through efforts to bring about openness of mind and will to the demands of the common good is something which concerns the Church deeply.[12]

In Pope Benedict's words, we see again the tension between faith and politics. It is not the purpose of the Church to make society just. That is the role of the state. But the state cannot make society just if it is not informed by truth. Communicating that truth is the role of the Church. The Church's social doctrine, therefore, both shapes the souls of her members and models justice for the larger society.

In this doctrine "politics and faith meet," Pope Benedict explains. "Faith ... is an encounter with the living God — an encounter opening up new horizons extending beyond the sphere of reason. ... Faith enables reason to do its work more effectively and to see its proper object more clearly."[13] Tension is not opposition. Rather, it is the strength that unites the complementary purposes of the Church and government. "This is where Catholic social doctrine has its place," Benedict explains; "it has no intention of giving the Church power over the State." Rather, the Church's "aim is simply to help purify reason and to contribute, here and now, to the acknowledgment and attainment of what is just."[14]

The Church wishes to help form consciences in political life and to stimulate greater insight into the authentic requirements of justice as well as greater readiness to act accordingly. ... Building a just social and civil order, wherein each person receives what is his or her due, is an essential task which every generation must take up anew. As a political task, this cannot be the Church's immediate responsibility. Yet, since it is also a most important human responsibility, the Church is duty-bound to offer, through the purification of reason and through ethical formation, her own specific contribution towards understanding the requirements of justice and achieving them politically.[15]

Pope Benedict connects this demand for public justice with the virtue of charity. "The specific expressions of ecclesial charity can never be confused with the activity of the State," he explains. But "charity must animate the entire lives of the lay faithful and therefore also their political activity, lived as 'social charity.'"[16] The charity that animates the lives of the lay faithful is expressed through the mediating civic structures that fall under the principle of subsidiarity.

Civic Duty, Politics, and Subsidiarity

Beginning in 2007, in anticipation of each even-year national election, the United States Conference of Catholic Bishops has released variations on a teaching document called "Forming Consciences for Faithful Citizenship: A Call to Political Responsibility from the Catholic Bishops of the United States."[17] The current version is substantially unchanged from the one released in 2015, in anticipation of the 2016 election. The purpose of the document is not to tell Catholics how to vote, but rather to inform the faithful about their civic responsibility, and the

Church's understanding of a broad range of policy issues, so that we may make an informed decision about how we cast our votes. Of course, few elections in American history have been more vexing and divisive than the presidential elections from 2016 onward. Clear instruction about civic responsibility and substantive issues has never been more urgent, and "Forming Consciences" is important for that purpose. In reading this document, it is important to have a clear understanding of the critical distinction between our broad duty of participation in *civic* life and the narrower responsibility for *political* activity.

Political life is but one of many subdivisions of broad, robust civic life. An abundant civic life also includes membership and activity in fraternal organizations, community groups, social clubs, ecclesial ministries, sports teams, and other associations of persons. Our responsibility to engage in civic life usually includes political obligations, but the far more important activity is found in these smaller, closer subsidiary associations that aid in the development and fulfillment of the human person. Indeed, political life should be ordered toward these nonpolitical aspects of civic life, creating and sustaining the conditions by which they may flourish. The measure of politics is its effectiveness in minimizing its direct role in people's lives as it maximizes the conditions for the proliferation of nonpolitical subsidiary structures. But this principle makes a demand on us: In our consideration of public life, we must not elevate politics to a level that it should not have. This includes having a more cautious and circumspect approach to how we cast a vote in elections and referenda.

For many, if not most, of us, the most common political activity in which we engage is voting. Yet, as seen in the context of recent presidential elections, we may sometimes find ourselves in the position of having to cast a vote for one of two morally unfit candidates. By reaffirming the priority of the broader concept of civic life over the narrow one of political life, we can imagine ways to be responsible citizens even when we cannot cast a vote for either candidate in good conscience. Political life and responsible citizenship are related, but they are not the same thing. Politics is but one of many expressions of civic friendship. The *Catechism* refers to the obligation of broader civic "participation," defined as "voluntary and generous engagement ... in social interchange" (1913). This is achieved "first of all" not in political terms, but rather "by taking charge of the areas for which one assumes *personal responsibility*: by the care taken for the education of his family, by conscientious work, and so forth" (1914). The "so forth" should be understood as those numerous intermediary institutions that constitute civic life, but have nothing to do with politics: for example, community soccer leagues; benevolent organizations like the St. Vincent de Paul Society or Knights of Columbus; local soup kitchens, food pantries, or clothes closets. Tending to domestic duties, in other words, is participation in civic friendship. These, rather than political activity, are the *primary* means of exercising the obligations of civic life.

Only after accounting for this primary obligation of broad civic obligation does the *Catechism* state that "as far as possible citizens should take an active part in *public life*" (1915), which presumably may include political activity. This way of accounting for the obligations of citizenship is an expression of subsidiarity. To reduce the obligations of civic friendship to political life is to miss this essential aspect of Catholic social teaching. Moreover, it distorts our understanding of where the primary exercise of citizenship lies: in the myriad social organizations that exist apart from, and more closely to our lives than, politics. To equate civic responsibility with political life reduces citizenship to political activity. This, in turn, leads to the dubious conclusion that one has a moral obligation to participate in political life by, for example, voting. The moral obligation is to participate in civic life. How — or whether — we vote in a particular election of constrained choices is a matter of prudential judgment within the broader moral obligation of civic life.

By no means am I suggesting that voting is optional, or that the moral obligations of citizenship do not extend to voting. Usually, the moral obligations of citizenship do include voting, but they might not. If the narrow range of voting choices in a particular election forces us to cast a vote that does not contribute to the common good, it may very well be the case that refraining from casting a ballot is the more responsible act of civic friendship. This is because the Christian vocation is not to effect social change, as Pope Benedict reminds us, but rather to witness to the truth of the Gospel. And if casting a vote cannot be consistent with the integrity of that witness, it may be that voting is a violation of the obligations of citizenship, not its necessary corollary. In those cases, the option more consistent with our civic obligation to witness to truth may be to abstain from checking either box on a given ballot. Of course, the option of writing in another candidate is also available. While I do not gainsay this option, it is almost always tantamount to abstaining. But writing in is still consistent with my suggestion: We should not feel morally obligated to choose one of two unfit candidates put forward by the two political parties that monopolize the ballot.

In this context, we must keep in mind the admonition of Saint Paul that we may never choose the "lesser" of two evil options so that some perceived good may come. "And why not say … that we should do evil that good may come of it?" (Rom 3:8). Answering his own question, he says that a person who advocates this deserves condemnation. When we are faced with two evil choices in an election, we may not justify casting a vote for the lesser evil because we think it will be a vote "against" the greater. To will a (lesser) evil choice is to will evil. This we may *never* do. We may not form an intention to choose evil that some "good" may come, even if that good is to vote against a greater evil. If we have reached the conscientious decision that our vote for either of two candidates is a vote for a lesser evil, we may not cast a vote for either candidate. This may bring us face-to-face with how we consider our partisan political commitment. We may not allow our partisan loyalty to trump our moral obligation not to choose evil. Thus we may not cast a vote that we consider to be the lesser of two evils merely because that candidate is a member of our party. This is to elevate politics over faith, the very definition of idolatry.

I am not suggesting that a Catholic cannot have cast a vote in good conscience in past elections, or that she cannot in upcoming ones. Certainly, the judgment of anyone else's conscience is outside my competence. I am suggesting, however, that we should not engage in moral contortions to justify a vote for a morally unfit candidate out of a mistaken notion that we are always morally obligated to vote. It may be that the decision most consistent with the Gospel, and thus of conscientious contribution to the common good, is to stand as a witness that neither party's candidate is worthy of our vote. This may also be an opportunity to demonstrate the broader false choice of the two versions of liberalism represented by the two major parties. This is not an abdication of citizenship, but the most morally consistent expression of it. And if we have reached the conclusion that both votes would be a vote for evil, we may not cast a vote for either.

Our civic obligation is not to participate in party politics, but rather to witness to the truth of the Gospel, including its expression in the Church's social doctrine. Again, I am most certainly not making a blanket assertion that a Catholic cannot vote or otherwise participate in American political life. I have voted in every election for at least the past twenty years or so.

But I have sometimes refrained from completing a ballot if some choices necessarily entailed choosing a lesser evil over a greater one. We should not be constrained to choose one evil option over another evil option under some misconceived notion that we have an obligation to cast a complete ballot in every election. The obverse, of course, is that we do not violate any moral obligation by abstaining from a vote in certain circumstances. On the contrary, in some cases that may be the better moral choice — or even the only good one.

This is also a reminder that politics is the lower form of social and civic life. The primary focus of our civic lives of "social charity," as Pope Benedict puts it, should not be national, or even state and local, elections. Rather, it should be on those "helping" institutions that are closer to public needs and the goods that meet them. With this focus, we not only contribute to our more immediate neighbors, but we witness to the truth of subsidiarity as a mandate of Catholic moral life. And we stand as a witness against the falsehood that responsible citizenship can only be exercised by identification with one of the two liberal parties in American politics. It is not difficult to imagine — indeed we do not have to imagine — situations in which participation in either of these parties is inconsistent with Catholic witness.

This raises serious questions of how, or whether, a Catholic can be a patriot in the context of American politics.

Is Patriotism Possible in the United States?

The United States was established upon a set of moral doctrines, rather than a common ethnic or demographic heritage — perhaps unique in the history of the world at the time of our country's founding. Of course, the population represented by the Continental Congress, which was not everyone who lived in what became the United States, broadly shared a common language and ethnic heritage. But this was not the basis for the new nation. By its own confession, the United States was founded upon a moral theory, not a shared demographic, racial, or linguistic community. It is difficult to overstate how important this is for a consideration of the attribute — or even possibility — of patriotism. The nature of the founding has at least three implications for the way we Catholics might understand both citizenship and patriotism.

The first implication is that patriotism may not even be the right name for an attitude of loyalty to the United States. In 1984, Alasdair MacIntyre gave the annual Lindley Lecture at the University of Kansas, entitled "Is Patriotism a Virtue?" For my purpose, his answer is not why the lecture is relevant. Rather, MacIntyre raises the question of whether patriotism is even an intelligible category in the United States. He defines patriotism as "a kind of loyalty to a particular nation which only those possessing that particular nationality can exhibit."[18] This definition would exclude patriotism as a category that can even apply to American loyalty. Arguably, other than displaced and dispossessed indigenous peoples, we Americans do not "share a particular nationality." Even though often many generations removed, we are a country of disparate nationalities. Loyalties to these heritages often make greater moral and sentimental claims upon us than our identities as American citizens. This is not, of course, to suggest that we Americans cannot exhibit an attitude toward the United States that has many of the same qualities as patriotism and its attendant characteristics, such as loyalty and service. But it is difficult to call it patriotism.

In contrast to patriotism, MacIntyre suggests an "attitude" by which people are "protagonists of their own nation's causes because and only because, so they assert, it is their nation which is the champion of some great moral ideal" (emphasis his). This includes Americans "who claim that the United States deserves our allegiance because it champions the goods of freedom against the evils of communism."[19] With a qualification discussed below, I am somewhat sympathetic with MacIntyre's definition of patriotism, as well as his contrast between patriotism and whatever we might call the attitude that he associates with loyalty to the moral principles enumerated in the Declaration of Independence. This is not to say that we Americans are not capable of patriot-like impulses. Nor is it to suggest that the United States is devoid of attributes that are the proper objects of those impulses. But MacIntyre's argument complicates how we think about those loyalties, especially as Catholic Christians.

For the purpose of this book, MacIntyre's taxonomy is also complicated because it seems to conflict with theories of patriotism articulated by, for example, Pope St. John Paul II. MacIntyre's definition of patriotism may be more like chauvinism or a certain kind of nationalism, which John Paul distinguished from a proper definition of legitimate patriotism. For example, the Pope contrasts "an unhealthy form of nationalism, which teaches contempt for other nations or cultures" with patriotism, "which is a proper love of one's country." Properly speaking, "patriotism never seeks to advance the well-being of one's own nation at the expense of others," he continues. "Nationalism ... is thus the antithesis of true patriotism."[20]

In his final book, John Paul expanded this discussion by his discussion of patria, defined as "the values and spiritual content that make up the culture of a given nation."[21] He explains that the shared culture that forms a nation is the indication that the nation is a "natural society, not the mere product of convention," such as the "State."[22] As such, however, the nation cannot be identified with a "so-called democratic society," he cautions. "Democratic society is closer to the State than is the nation," he concludes.[23]

Of course, I embrace this distinction. The problem, however, is that it may be difficult to call the United States a nation in the way the Pope defines the term. Indeed, the United States looks more like a conventional state than a natural nation. This is why, even while affirming Pope John Paul II's important teaching, MacIntyre's discussion is still relevant to my argument.

This brings us to the second implication of the unique founding of the United States. John Paul suggests that the nation is the natural foundation on which conventional states are built, in order to preserve the common culture.[24] But my argument is that the United States has no such ground because it has no shared culture to define it as a nation. If the United States is not a true nation, then — to return to the subhead of this chapter — is patriotism even possible? Citizenship is certainly possible in a nationless state. But is patriotism, at least as defined and advocated by Pope St. John Paul II?

Because no linguistic, ethnic, racial, or other inherent demographic characteristic is intrinsic to commitment to the United States, no one is naturally excluded from either citizenship or the possibility of patriot-like loyalty. (I say "naturally" excluded because, of course, criteria for citizenship may be established by legislation. Even so, U.S. citizenship is defined by commitment to a set of ideas and the nation that purports to uphold them.) Commitment to a moral idea does not require that you speak a certain language, share a particular ethnic heritage, or have a certain skin shade. Loyalty is intellectual assent to a set of moral propositions and the regime that protects them. It is a voluntary, contractual agreement, unconstrained by any sense of natural bonds or allegiances. One can withdraw consent for any or no reason. One cannot change one's ethnic heritage, however. Thus the kinds of inchoate attachments to heritage or cultural esteem that attend more traditional forms of national patriotism are not a part of American loyalty or devotion. No sense of national pride plays a role in intellectual commitment.

Over the course of its nearly 250 years, the United States has developed a highly complex and diversified body of political, legal, and regulatory institutions. Many people consider this progress to be consistent with the moral principles of the founding, properly understood through a lens of historical development. I'll call this the "Development Theory." From the perspective of the Development Theory, the growth of government is a necessary corollary of the protection of our unalienable rights. And, of course, adherents to the Development Theory believe that we may discover, indeed, that we have discovered additional particular rights that are at least consistent with the general rights enumerated in the Declaration of Independence and (later) the U.S. Constitution. Loyalty to the founding principles, therefore, demands loyalty to the growth of the laws and regulations that protect the developing body of rights. From the perspective of the Development Theory, people who dissent from the current state of affairs are really rejecting the founding principles. These dissenters would be considered unpatriotic to their progressive adversaries, the development theorists.

In the view of many others, however, growth of these legal and regulatory institutions has come at the cost of betraying the moral theory at the nation's founding. I'll call this the "Corruption Theory." One might subscribe to the original moral doctrine but determine that the United States has compromised, perverted, or abandoned that doctrine. When this occurs, loyalty to the United States is perfectly consistent with harsh criticism of the prevailing state of affairs. In the view of the corruption theorists, in fact, authentic loyalty demands condemnation of those institutions that are not consistent with the founding principles as they understand them. One is not disloyal to the nation, in such a case, but rather critical of its abandonment of the ideals upon which it was founded and which it continues to profess. For the corruption theorists, the development theorists are disloyal because these developments are not consistent with founding principles.

Of course, this is not an exhaustive taxonomy of attitudes about the founding or the growth of the federal government and its regulatory agencies. There are variations on the theme — for example, that it was a bad idea at the beginning. Some criticize the Development Theory, but do not subscribe to the Corruption Theory. Others celebrate the Corruption Theory, but precisely because, in their view, the founding principles should have been abandoned for something else. This is not the place to treat these variations. It is enough, however, to point out that they further complicate what it means to be patriotic to a country founded upon consent to an idea rather than organic national identity.

But *Can* Everyone Consent?

This brings me to the third implication of the United States being founded upon a moral idea rather than a set of natural attachments. Must one agree with that idea to be a loyal American? If the United States is founded upon a moral theory (or set of moral principles), can one have patriot-like attitudes if one does not give intellectual assent to the theory or principles? If the theory is all there is, and one dissents from the theory, what is left? Does it leave one politically homeless — or worse, a traitor? And if that is the case, what posture should one take to questions of citizenship and loyalty to national interests?

This is not idle conjecture. In recent years, a considerable developing body of political philosophy has called into question the very legitimacy of the individualist moral philosophy at the heart of the American founding. Proponents of these theories — sometimes called "integralism" or (more broadly) "post-liberalism" — argue that the moral and political ideals upon which the United States is founded are inconsistent with a Catholic understanding of the human person.[24] The moral anthropology of individual rights is in tension, if not incompatible, with the Catholic understandings of solidarity and common good. Of course, by now the reader of this book knows that I am sympathetic with this argument. If this is the case — if the United States is founded upon the rejection of the most fundamental principles of Catholic moral theology — is it possible for a Catholic to be a loyal citizen at all? Or must Catholics live as aliens in the very place we call home?

Rejecting the moral principles of the founding does not mean that we have to reject every political, legal, regulatory, or even cultural institution that has grown over the last two-and-a-half centuries. Good institutions may emerge despite the moral or philosophical obstacles that impede them. One is not necessarily "anti-American" if one has fundamental philosophical or theological objections to the moral foundations of the country. More importantly, good people can rise above even bad principles. But since, as I have suggested in this book, the moral theory of the founding is contradictory to the Catholic doctrine of the human person, we should not be surprised when the theory is corrosive of the doctrine. If that is the case, suspicious vigilance rather than affirmative loyalty should be our fundamental posture toward America.

Moreover, even if one disagrees with the integralist or post-liberal schools (or any other Catholic criticism of the American regime), their critiques are important for all Catholics who are concerned about the possibilities and limitations of patriot-like loyalty to this or any nation. Catholics must always be vigilant about commitment to *anything* that is not the Gospel. We must continue to grapple with questions about the compatibility of the Catholic Faith and the principles at the heart of the American founding. Regardless of how we lean toward an answer, when we forget or ignore the questions, we expose ourselves to idolatry, because the less aware we are of idols, the more likely we are to bow down to them. When it comes to our lives as Americans, we often fall when we forget the critical distinction between loyalty to nation and faithfulness to the Gospel.

Pragmatic Loyalty and Articles of Peace

What, then, is a Catholic to make of America if, as this book has proposed, the moral and political theories that animate it are largely contradictory to the Catholic Faith? For a tentative proposal, I return to the famous American priest and political theorist John Courtney Murray, SJ, and his book *We Hold These Truths: Catholic Reflections on the American Proposition*.

As Father Murray observed, we should not ask whether Catholicism is compatible with the principles of America's founding. Instead, we must invert the question: "It must, of course, be turned round to read, whether American democracy is compatible with Catholicism."[26] Murray's formulation is helpful for our consideration of the problem of loyalty to the United States, but it does not end the discussion or resolve the conundrum.

Even if American democracy is compatible with Catholicism, it does not necessarily follow that Catholics should — or even can — be patriots, even if by analogy. For example, we might conclude that there are aspects of the American political founding that, on balance, do not make the United States fundamentally hostile to Catholic faith and practice, even if they are inconsistent with Catholic moral principles. But this hardly inspires patriotic devotion. It may, however, be the best we can do in admiring and even embracing the good traditions and institutions of American political life while preserving the integrity of our witness as Christian disciples.

We Catholics should try to reimagine patriotism as a pragmatic compromise. This allows us to be good citizens, participating in the social and political life of the nation to the extent that such participation is compatible with our Faith. It allows us sincerely to celebrate aspects of American political life that are not inconsistent with Christian discipleship. We might even find aspects of the moral theory at the heart of the founding that we can advance in good faith. But we will never fully embrace unqualified patriotic devotion. To do so would be to collapse the critical distance and divert the wary eye that we must always maintain, so that we do not confuse being a good American with being a faithful Christian. Perhaps we can be both. But they are not the same thing. And as faithful Christians we must always be witness to the conflicts inherent in our American loyalty.

Father Murray suggests that we should consider the moral principles of the American founding as "articles of peace" rather than "articles of faith," framing his discussion around the specific rights enumerated in the First Amendment to the U.S. Constitution. Some people read into the First Amendment "certain ultimate beliefs ... with regard to the nature of religion, religious truth, the church, faith, conscience, divine revelation, human freedom, etc.," he suggests. "In this view these articles ... are dogmas, norms of orthodoxy, to which one must conform on pain of some manner of excommunication," he continues. "They are true articles of faith. Hence it is necessary to believe them, to give them a religiously motivated assent."[27] This is not to suggest that these people all agree with the practical implications of their faith. "Those who dogmatize about these articles do not usually do so with all the clarity that dogmas require," Murray drolly observes.[28]

Not surprisingly, Murray argues that Catholics cannot embrace the moral and political principles of the First Amendment (and the more general doctrines of which they are species) as articles of faith. "The only tenable position" is that these principles "are not articles of faith but articles of peace. ... They are not true dogma but only good law. That is praise enough," Father Murray contends. "This, I take it, is the Catholic view."[29] Of course, some may disagree even that these political principles are "good law." But Murray's suggestion that we take the moral principles as articles of peace is helpful for understanding that we may live (uneasily) on the moral foundations of the United States, but we can never really embrace them with unbridled enthusiasm.

Indeed, I believe that we *must* heed Father Murray's conclusion that taking these principles as articles of peace is the "Catholic view." Too many of us uncritically embrace the moral foundations of the United States without doing the hard work of asking whether or to what extent they are in tension with Catholic doctrine. Even worse, some believe and argue that the founding principles should be embraced as articles of faith, as though they are divinely inspired corollaries of Christian moral theology. As I suggested throughout this book, this is a dangerous — and perhaps idolatrous — game. But it is one that we see played out in our current political culture.

As I come to the end of this book, I suggest that we take a step back to consider both the demands of the doctrines of our faith and the competing demands of American citizenship. Perhaps the demands can be reconciled. And by no means am I suggesting categorically that they cannot. But if they can be reconciled, something like Father Murray's distinction between articles of faith and peace is the necessary approach. We do not take the moral theories of the American founding as theological principles, but as pragmatically workable propositions for living peaceable lives in a pluralist political culture. If we conceive of it this way, we can be America's good civic friends, but God's faithful servants first.

Acknowledgments

I am thankful to my present and past students in MT 600 — Catholic Social Doctrine, who have cheerfully endured the rehearsal of this book in the classroom and charitably helped me to sharpen its arguments. I also express my heartfelt gratitude to my editor, Mary Beth Giltner. She has gently called out those places where I have been unclear and challenged me to speak a language that is more comprehensible for the reader. Where the book fails in this, the fault lies with my obduracy rather than Mary Beth's skill and patience. Finally, I am continually grateful to my family — my wife, Sue, and nine children — who are living testimony to the fullness of the Catholic moral life.

Notes

CHAPTER 1
We Are All Liberal Protestants

1. Patrick O'Brian, *The Nutmeg of Consolation*, in *The Complete Aubrey/Maturin Novels, Books 13–16* (New York: W. W. Norton and Co., Inc., 2004), 4661.

2. Ibid., 4668.

3. Ibid., 4672.

4. Ibid., 4674.

5. Ibid., 4674.

6. Ibid., 4674.

7. O'Brian, *The Commodore*, in *The Complete Aubrey/Maturin Novels, Books 17–21* (New York: W. W. Norton and Co., Inc., 2004), 5353.

8. Alasdair MacIntyre, *After Virtue*, 3rd ed. (Notre Dame: University of Notre Dame Press, 2007), 1.

9. Ibid., 1.

10. Ibid., 2.

11. Augustine of Hippo, *On Reprimand and Grace* 1.2, in *On the Free Choice of the Will, On Grace and Free Choice, and Other Writings*, ed. and trans. Peter King (Cambridge: Cambridge University Press, 2010), 186.

12. John Paul II, Homily, October 8, 1995, vatican.va, par. 7.

13. Thomas Hobbes, *Leviathan: The Matter, Form and Power of a Commonwealth Ecclesiastical and Civil*, 14.2.

14. Ibid., 14.1.

15. Ibid., 14.4 (emphasis added).

16. Ibid., 13.13.

17. Ibid.

18. Ibid., 14.8.

19. Ibid.

20. Planned Parenthood of Southeastern Pennsylvania v. Casey, 505 U.S. 833, 851 (1992).

21. Augustine of Hippo, *The Literal Meaning of Genesis*, vol. 2, trans. John Hammond Taylor, SJ (New York: The Newman Press, 1982), bk. 11, chap. 15, par. 20, p. 147.

22. Augustine of Hippo, *The City of God*, trans. Marcus Dods (New York: Random House, 1950), bk. 14, chap. 28, p. 477.

23. Augustine, *The Literal Meaning of Genesis*, bk. 11, chap. 15, par. 20, p. 147.

24. Ibid.

25. *The Epistle to Diognetus*, chap. 5, excerpt taken from vatican.va.

26. Ibid.

27. Francis, *Fratelli Tutti*, vatican.va., par. 99.

28. John Courtney Murray, SJ, *We Hold These Truths: Catholic Reflections on the American Proposition* (New York: Sheed and Ward, 1960), ix–x.

29. Ibid., xi.

30. Ibid.

31. Ibid.

32. Stanley Hauerwas, *A Community of Character* (Notre Dame: University of Notre Dame Press, 1991), chap. 4.

33. Ibid.

CHAPTER 2
Creation, Fall, and Alienation: How We Forgot That We Are Social Beings

1. Jessica Hooten Wilson, *Reading for the Love of God: How to Read as a Spiritual Practice* (Grand Rapids, MI: Baker Publishing Group, 2023).

2. Ibid.

3. Ibid.

4. Ibid.

5. Augustine, *The Literal Meaning of Genesis*, vol. 1, trans. John Hammond Taylor, SJ (Mahwah, NJ: Paulist Press, 1982), bk. 1, chap. 1, par. 1, p. 19.

6. My point is summarized in the Dogmatic Constitution on Divine Revelation (*Dei Verbum*) from the Second Vatican Council: "To search out the intention of the sacred writers, attention should be given, among other things, to 'literary forms.' For truth is set forth and expressed differently in texts which are variously historical, prophetic, poetic, or of other forms of discourse. The interpreter must investigate what meaning the sacred writer intended to express and actually expressed in particular circumstances by using contemporary literary forms in accordance with the situation of his own time and culture. For the correct understanding of what the sacred author wanted to assert, due attention must be paid to the customary and characteristic styles of feeling, speaking and narrating which prevailed at the time of the sacred writer, and to the patterns men normally employed at that period in their everyday dealings with one another.", vatican.va., par. 12.

7. See Genesis 1:3 and 5, 6 and 8, 9 and 13, 14 and 19, 20 and 23, 24 and 31.

8. As John Bergsma and Brant Pitre explain it in *A Catholic Introduction to the Bible, Volume 1: The Old Testament* (San Francisco: Ignatius Press, 2018), 97, God first creates three realms, and then three corre-

sponding rulers, culminating with man, who rules over all.

9. Joseph Ratzinger, *"In the Beginning …": A Catholic Understanding of the Story of Creation and the Fall,* trans. Boniface Ramsey, OP (Grand Rapids, MI: Eerdmans, 1995), 28.

10. Augustine of Hippo, *Confessions,* trans. Thomas Williams (Indianapolis: Hackett Publishing Co., 2019), bk. 7, chap. 12, par. 18, p. 111.

11. Augustine, *The City of God,* bk. 11, chap. 9, p. 354.

12. See, generally, Thomas Aquinas, *Summa Theologiae,* I-II, q.6.

13. Ratzinger, *"In the Beginning …",* 47.

14. Ibid., 48.

15. This translation is from Robert Alter, *The Hebrew Bible, Volume 1: The Five Books of Moses* (New York: W.W. Norton and Co., 2019), 15. Alter explains that "the subordinate conjunction that introduces the serpent's first utterance does not have the sense of 'truly' that most translators assign it, and is better construed as the beginning of a (false) statement that is cut off in midsentence by Eve's objection that the ban is not on *all* the trees of the Garden." Alter, *The Hebrew Bible, Volume 1,* n. 2.

16. Ibid.,18.

17. Ratzinger, *"In the Beginning …",* 71.

18. Ibid.

CHAPTER 3
A Better Foundation: Catholic Social Doctrine

1. Pontifical Council for Justice and Peace, *Compendium of the Social Doctrine of the Church,* accessed October 4, 2023, vatican.va, par. 111.

2. Second Vatican Council, *Gaudium et Spes,* vatican.va, par. 12..

3. Pontifical Council for Justice and Peace, *Compendium of the Social Doctrine of the Church,* par. 117.

4. Ibid., quoting John Paul II, *Reconciliatio et Paenitentia,* vatican.va, par. 16.

5. Leo XIII, *Rerum Novarum,* vatican.va.

6. Walker Percy, *The Moviegoer* (New York: Vintage International, 1998), 11.

7. Ibid.

8. Ibid.

9. Ibid., 13.

10. Walker Percy, *Lost in the Cosmos: The Last Self-Help Book* (New York: Picador, 1983), 7.

11. Ibid., 11.

12. Ibid., 12.

13. Friedrich Nietzsche, "On Use and Abuse of History for Life," in *The Untimely Meditations,* trans. Anthony Ludovici and Adrian Collins, Pantianos Classics, Apple eBook ed., 130 (emphasis added).

14. Ibid.

15. John Paul II, *Evangelium Vitae,* vatican.va, par. 18.

16. John Paul II, *Sollicitudo Rei Socialis,* vatican.va, par. 38.

17. Francis, *Fratelli Tutti,* par. 116.

18. John Paul II, *Sollicitudo Rei Socialis,* par. 38, citing Mt 10:40–42; 20:25; Mk 10:42–45; Lk 22:25–27.

19. Second Vatican Council, *Gaudium et Spes,* par. 22.

20. John Paul II, General Audience, February 10, 1988, par. 9–10, https://www.ewtn.com/catholicism/library/jesus-friend-of-sinners-23917.

21. Pius XI, *Quadragesimo Anno,* vatican.va, par. 79.

22. Ibid., par. 80.

23. For a general discussion of this irony, see Patrick Deneen, *Why Liberalism Failed* (New Haven, CT: Yale University Press, 2019).

24. Pius XI, *Quadragesimo Anno,* par. 79.

25. Second Vatican Council, *Gaudium et Spes,* par. 74.

CHAPTER 4
The Family as the First Subsidiarity Society

1. The group is composed of prominent solo artists Amanda Shires, Brandi Carlile, Natalie Hemby, and Maren Morris. "Crowded Table" was written by Brandi Carlile and Natalie Hemby, with Lori McKenna.

2. Second Vatican Council, *Gaudium et Spes,* par. 12.

3. John Paul II, *Familiaris Consortio*, vatican.va, par. 18.

4. Ibid., par. 18, 43.

5. Ibid., par. 18.

6. Ibid., par. 46.

7. Ibid., par. 43.

8. Pius XI, *Divini Illius Magistri*, vatican.va, par. 11.

9. Ibid., par. 12.

10. Russell Hittinger, "The Three Necessary Societies," *First Things*, June 2017, https://www.firstthings.com/article/2017/06/the-three-necessary-societies.

11. John Paul II, *Familiaris Consortio*, par. 18.

12. Ibid., par. 17.

13. Ibid., par. 36.

14. Ibid., par. 42.

15. Ibid.

16. Ibid.

17. Ibid., par. 43.

18. Pontifical Council for Justice and Peace, *Compendium of the Social Doctrine of the Church*, par. 252.

19. John Paul II, *Evangelium Vitae*, par. 11.

20. Ibid.

21. Ibid.

22. Paul VI, *Humanae Vitae*, vatican.va, par. 1.

23. Second Vatican Council, *Gaudium et Spes*, par. 48.

24. Elizabeth Breunig, "Make Birth Free: It's Time the Pro-life Movement Chose Life," *The Atlantic*, July 9, 2022, https://www.theatlantic.com/ideas/archive/2022/07/post-roe-pro-life-parental-support/661473/.

25. Catherine Glenn Foster and Kristen Day, *Make Birth Free: A Vision for Congress to Empower American Mothers, Families, and Communities* (Washington, D.C.: Americans United for Life, 2023), https://aul.org/wp-content/uploads/2023/01/Make-Birth-Free-White-Paper.pdf.

26. These data compare countries composing the Organization for Economic Co-operation and Development, a consortium of thirty-eight

high-income to very high-income countries from North America, western and central Europe, and parts of Asia, including Israel, Japan, South Korea, Australia, and New Zealand, https://www.oecd.org.

27. Justina Petrullo, "US Has Highest Infant, Maternal Mortality Rates Despite the Most Health Care Spending," *American Journal of Managed Care,* January 31, 2023. All data in this paragraph are taken from this article, https://www.ajmc.com/view/us-has-highest-infant-maternal-mortality-rates-despite-the-most-health-care-spending.

28. Foster and Day, "Make Birth Free," 2–3.

29. Ibid., 3.

30. Breunig, "Make Birth Free."

31. Foster and Day, "Make Birth Free," 3.

32. Bianca Pallaro and Alicia Parlapiano, "Four Ways to Understand the $54 Billion in U.S. Spending in Ukraine," *New York Times,* May 20, 2022, https://www.nytimes.com/interactive/2022/05/20/upshot/ukraine-us-aid-size.html.

33. For a sympathetic critique of Foster and Day, see Leah Libresco Sargeant and Patrick T. Brown, "Making It Easier to Have a Child Doesn't Require Making Birth Free," Institute for Family Studies, January 23, 2023, https://ifstudies.org/blog/making-it-easier-to-have-a-child-doesnt-require-making-birth-free.

34. For additional consideration of the economics of our current system compared to a proposed free birth regime, see Robert Orr, "Yes, Birth Should be Free," Institute for Family Studies, February 8, 2023, https://ifstudies.org/blog/yes-birth-should-be-free.

35. Paul VI, *Humanae Vitae*, par. 10.

36. Alasdair MacIntyre, *Dependent Rational Animals* (Chicago: Open Court, 1999), 1.

CHAPTER 5
Work: Where Dignity and Solidarity Meet

1. Leo XIII, *Rerum Novarum*, par. 1.

2. Ibid., par. 2.

3. John Paul II, *Laborem Exercens*, vatican.va.

4. Ibid., par. 1.

5. Ibid., par. 4.

6. Booker T. Washington, *Up from Slavery: An Autobiography* (Garden City, NY: Doubleday, Page and Co., Inc., 1901), 148.

7. Ibid., 72.

8. Ibid.

9. Ibid.

10. Ibid.

11. Ibid., 73.

12. Ibid., 149.

13. Ibid., 148.

14. Ibid., 74.

15. John Paul II, *Laborem Exercens*, par. 9.

16. Ibid.

17. Ibid.

18. Washington, *Up from Slavery*, 74.

19. Ibid.

20. Ibid., 154.

21. Joseph Pieper, *Leisure: The Basis of Culture*, trans. Alexander Dru (San Francisco: Ignatius Press, 2009), Kindle, 48.

22. Ibid.

23. Ibid., 50.

24. John Paul II, *Laborem Exercens*, par. 12.

25. Second Vatican Council, *Gaudium et Spes*, par. 67.

26. Leo XIII, *Rerum Novarum*, par. 49.

27. See Kenneth Craycraft, "Gritty and Gripping: 'On the Waterfront' Still Speaks a Godly Truth," *Our Sunday Visitor*, September 4, 2023, https://www.osvnews.com/2023/09/04/gritty-and-gripping-on-the-waterfront-still-speaks-a-godly-truth/.

28. John Paul II, *Laborem Exercens*, par. 20.

29. Leo XIII, *Rerum Novarum*, par. 49.

30. Second Vatican Council, *Gaudium et Spes*, par. 67.

31. J. Brian Benestad, *Church, State, and Society: An Introduction to Catholic Social Doctrine* (Washington, D.C.: The Catholic University of America Press, 2011), 156–159. Benestad draws upon Petro Pavan and Teodoro Onofri, *La Dottrina Sociale Cristiana*, 3rd ed. (Rome: An. Veritatis, 1966).

32. Ibid., 332–333.

33. Ibid., 333.

CHAPTER 6
Economic Life: Money, Markets, and Morality

1. Leo XIII, *Rerum Novarum*, par. 15.

2. Pius XI, *Quadragesimo Anno*, par. 117.

3. Ibid., par. 120.

4. Ibid., par. 107, 118.

5. John Paul II, *Sollicitudo Rei Socialis*, par. 21.

6. John Paul II, *Centesimus Annus*, vatican.va, par. 42.

7. Ibid.

8. Ibid.

9. Ibid., par. 43.

10. Second Vatican Council, *Gaudium et Spes*, par. 63.

11. John Paul II, *CA*, par. 32.

12. Ibid.

13. Ibid.

14. Ibid., par. 43.

15. Ibid., par. 39.

16. John Paul II, *Sollicitudo Rei Socialis*, par. 28.

17. John Paul II, *CA*, par. 48.

18. Ibid.

19. Ibid.

20. Ibid.

21. Ibid., par. 30.

22. John Paul II, *Sollicitudo Rei Socialis*, par. 42.

23. Ibid. (emphasis added).

CHAPTER 7
Political Life: Civic Friendship
and Christian Discipleship

1. Benedict XVI, Homily, October 16, 2011, vatican.va, quoting Augustine of Hippo, "Exposition on Psalms 4 and 94," Community of Hope, https://communityofhopeinc.org/Exposition%20of%20the%20Psalms.html.

2. Benedict XVI, Homily, October 16, 2011.

3. Augustine of Hippo, *On Free Choice*, in Ernest Fortin and Douglas Kries, eds., *Augustine: Political Writings*, trans. Michael W. Tkacz and Douglas Kries (Indianapolis: Hackett Publishing Co., 1994), bk. 1, chap. 5, par. 11–chap. 6, par. 15, p. 214.

4. Aquinas, *Summa Theologiae*, I-II, q.95, a.2.

5. Ibid., q.96, a.4.

6. Martin Luther King Jr., Letter from Birmingham Jail, April 16, 1963.

7. Ibid.

8. Ibid.

9. Benedict XVI, *Deus Caritas Est*, vatican.va, par. 28.

10. Ibid.

11. Ibid.

12. Ibid.

13. Ibid.

14. Ibid.

15. Ibid.

16. Ibid., par. 29.

17. United States Conference of Catholic Bishops, "Forming Consciences for Faithful Citizenship: A Call to Political Responsibility from the Catholic Bishops of the United States." The most recent version, issued for the 2022 and 2024 elections, was promulgated on January 20, 2020, https://www.usccb.org/issues-and-action/faithful-citizenship/upload/forming-consciences-for-faithful-citizenship.pdf.

18. Alasdair MacIntyre, "Is Patriotism a Virtue?" (Lindley Lecture, University of Kansas, March 26, 1984), 4.

19. Ibid., 3

20. Pope John Paul II, "Address to the Fiftieth General Assembly of the United Nations, October 5, 1995), paragraph 11. vatican.va/.

21. Pope John Paul II, *Memory and Identity: Conversations at the Dawn of a Mellennium* (New York: Rizzoli, 2005), 60.

22. Ibid., 69.

23. Ibid., 70.

24. Ibid.

25. See, for example, Deneen, *Why Liberalism Failed*, and Adriane Vermeule, *Common Good Constitutionalism* (Medford, MA: Polity Press, 2022).

26. Murray, We Hold These Truths, ix–x.

27. Ibid., 48–49.

28. Ibid., 49.

29. Ibid., 56.

About the Author

Kenneth Craycraft holds the James J. Gardner Family Chair in Moral Theology at Mount St. Mary's Seminary & School of Theology in Cincinnati. He is a regular columnist for *Our Sunday Visitor, OSV News, The Catholic Telegraph*, and the U.K. *Catholic Herald*. He has won multiple Catholic Press awards for general commentary for his "A Closer Look" column in *The Catholic Telegraph*. A licensed attorney, Dr. Craycraft holds the Ph.D. in theology from Boston College and the J.D. from Duke University School of Law. He is the author of *The American Myth of Religious Freedom* (Spence, 1999).